DISSENT *in* Dangerous Times

DISSENT *in* Dangerous Times

Edited by Austin Sarat

THE UNIVERSITY OF MICHIGAN PRESS
Ann Arbor

Published in the United States of America by
The University of Michigan Press
Printed and bound by CPI Group (UK) Ltd, Croydon, CR0 4YY

2008 2007 2006 2005 4 3 2 1

A CIP catalog record for this book is available from the British Library.

Library of Congress Cataloging-in-Publication Data

Dissent in dangerous times / edited by Austin Sarat.
p. cm.
Includes index.
ISBN13 978-0-472-09864-4 (cloth)
ISBN13 978-0-472-06864-7 (paper)
1. United States—Politics and government—2001– 2. Radicalism—United States. 3. Freedom of expression—United States. 4. Protest movements—United States. 5. Political culture—United States. 6. Political psychology. I. Sarat, Austin.

JK275.D57 2004
303.48'4—dc22 2004012108

ISBN13 978-0-472-09864-4 (cloth)
ISBN13 978-0-472-06864-7 (paper)
ISBN13 978-0-472-02552-7 (electronic)

I dedicate this book to my son, Benjamin,

with love and the hope that the world in which

he grows up will be a less dangerous one.

ACKNOWLEDGMENTS

The essays contained in this book were first presented at the Conference on Loyalty and Dissent in Dangerous Times, Amherst College, April 5–6, 2002. I am grateful to all those who participated in that event, in particular to Katherine Franke, Tom Dumm, Andrew Parker, Amrita Basu, Rebecca Stein, Frank Couvares, and Lawrence Douglas. I am also grateful for support, financial and otherwise, provided by Tom Gerety, former President of Amherst College, Lisa Raskin, former Dean of the Faculty, the Lecture Committee of Amherst College, and the Department of Law, Jurisprudence, and Social Thought. In this work, as in all that I do, I acknowledge the indispensable presence of my family. I thank them for their inspiration in helping me to see through, and beyond, dangerous times.

CONTENTS

TERRORISM, DISSENT, & REPRESSION: AN INTRODUCTION

Austin Sarat

> Will you fulfil the demands of the soul or will you yield yourself to the conventions of the world?
>
> —Ralph Waldo Emerson

> To those who scare peace-loving people with phantoms of lost liberty, my message is this: Your tactics only aid terrorists.
>
> —Attorney General John Ashcroft

> There are reminders to all Americans that they need to watch what they say, watch what they do, and this is not a time for remarks like that. There never is.
>
> —Ari Fleischer, *Press Secretary to President Bush, referring to remarks by comedian Bill Maher that the terrorists who destroyed the World Trade Center were not cowards*

> If in the name of security or of loyalty we start hacking away at our freedoms . . . , we will in the end forfeit security as well.
>
> —Henry Steele Commager

THE DANGERS OF DISSENT

Dissent is always dangerous to those who practice it and vexatious to those against whom it is directed. For both the dissenter and her target, dissent stirs up strong emotions and often calls forth strident reactions. Dissenters seek to define and occupy an in-between space, resistant to prevailing orthodoxy but engaged with it nonetheless. Even as she points out its flaws and demands redress, the dissenter affirms her continuing allegiance to the community she criticizes. The dissenter insists, as Henry Louis Gates puts it, that "critique can also be a form of commitment, a means of laying a claim. It's the ultimate gesture of citizenship. A way of saying: I'm not just passing through, I *live* here."[1]

The dissenter is neither conformist nor revolutionary. She is at once within, but outside of, the community and its conventions. In part because of her liminality the dissenter is often accused of disloyalty and subject to sanction and stigma by state and society. Pulled from the one side by those who say that dissent does not go far enough and from the other by those who demand acquiescence as the sign of loyalty, maintaining the "in-betweenness" of dissent is very difficult.[2]

Powerful people seldom appreciate challenge or embrace those who do not profess allegiance to their policies or practices. As Justice Oliver Wendell Holmes once wrote, "Persecution for the expression of opinions seems to me to be perfectly logical. If you have no doubt of your premises or your power and want a certain result with all your heart, you naturally express your wishes in law and sweep away all opposition."[3] Writing fifty years after Holmes, Justice William O. Douglas noted that government's "eternal temptation . . . has been to arrest the speaker rather than to correct the conditions about which he complains."[4]

While responses to dissent in state and society are contingent and historically specific, the general tendency is toward the containment, if not outright repression, of dissent. When the physical security of the community of which the dissenter is a member seems jeopardized, these tendencies and temptations intensify.[5] At such times the critic, the naysayer, the resister, who ordinarily is not welcomed warmly, comes under intense pressure to evacuate the space of dissent, to take sides, to choose allegiance over authenticity.

Despite this fact, dissent, that is, "speech that criticizes existing customs, habits, traditions, institutions, or authorities,"[6] has had a central and important role in America's national story and in our cultural imagination.[7] "From the beginning," Henry Steele Commager notes, "our own history was rooted in dissent."[8] Thus when we write history we treat the same dissenters who were condemned in their own time as heroes who bravely confronted power and changed history.[9] We inquire into the special psychology of the dissenter as hero,[10] even as we wonder whether we have the courage to stand up for what we believe.

In addition, dissent plays a significant role in legitimating our politics. Whatever the realities on the ground, recognizing a right to speak truth to power is advertised as a peculiarly American achievement.

Our freedoms, our cultural liveliness, these are the virtues that Americans most consistently use to explain what makes America distinct, special.[11] The political theorist George Kateb describes what he sees as a uniquely American kind of individualism, what he calls "democratic individuality," an individualism deeply entangled with dissent.[12] The democratic individual becomes a dissenter as an expression of "negative individuality," "the disposition to disobey bad conventions and unjust laws, by oneself, and on the basis of a strict moral self-scrutiny, self-examination," but also out of a commitment to "take responsibility for oneself—One's self must become a project, one must become the architect of one's soul."[13] Steven Shiffrin similarly identifies dissent's centrality to America's self-concept. Dissent, he says, is a "crucial institution for challenging unjust hierarchies and for promoting progressive change. It is also an important part of our national identity that we protect dissent."[14]

In this American story the dissenter is Everyman, moved to stand up against injustice, and the self of the dissenter is divided. It is a self desirous of the comfort that patriotism and loyalty provide, but ill at ease if the price of such comfort is silence in the face of the unjust suffering of others. In the American story dissent is part of a cultural politics, a cultural practice of engaging the question of injustice.[15] The spirit of dissent, so the story goes, permeates democratic culture. It should be affirmed, nurtured, fostered, not condemned and then tolerated. The call of dissent is, in Judith Butler's words, to hear "beyond what we are able to hear," to attend to an alterity whose presence is overwhelmed by events.[16]

However, as Holmes and Douglas remind us, American practices have often been quite at odds with these imaginings and aspirations. For example, Koffler and Gershman note that "the history of the First Amendment has been the history of intolerance of political dissent, a story of dark shadows of fear and orthodoxy illuminated periodically by brilliant rays of enlightenment."[17] Susan Ross argues that "despite nods to the vital role uninhibited debate plays in democratic self-governance, the Court has not consistently advanced a broad presumption against government action that encourages orthodoxy or discourages open discussion."[18]

Others argue that the picture is more complicated than Koffler and Gershman or Ross would have it, and that even as they discourage and domesticate dissent our institutions protect it as well. As Shiffrin puts it,

> The First Amendment serves to undermine dissent even as it protects it. Of course, the First Amendment protects dissent. It offers a legal claim for dissenters, and it functions as a cultural symbol encouraging dissenters to speak out. Nonetheless, the symbolism of the First Amendment perpetuates a cultural myth. It functions as a form of cultural ideology through which the society secures allegiance. It leads us to believe that America is the land of free speech, but it blinks at the "tyranny of the prevailing opinion and feeling," and it masks the extent to which free speech is marginalized, discouraged, and repressed. Even as it promotes dissent, it falsifies the willingness of the society to receive it, and it tolerates rules of place and property that make it difficult for people of modest means to address a mass audience.[19]

In the practices of our social and political institutions dissent is seldom celebrated and embraced. Most often dissent is accommodated into a defense of rights, in particular the right to freedom of expression. In this accommodation the emphasis is not on the dissenter but on dissent, not on the dissenter's heroic quality but on the value of tolerating dissent for our society. As a result, we are not enjoined to admire and imitate the dissenter, but only to "put up with" dissent. Dissent is an annoyance, maybe even an offense, but we respect the right to dissent even if we do not respect the dissenter. The best that the dissenter can expect is toleration,[20] a toleration that reassures those who express it of their own virtue while, at the same time, allowing them to condemn both those who dissent and the message they seek to communicate.

A striking example of such toleration is provided in a statement issued by the president of Amherst College after a flag-burning incident on the college's campus in October 2001. Five or six "outside agitators" appeared toward the end of an Assembly for Patriotism organized by Amherst students. These outsiders proceeded to burn an American flag.

In his statement, President Tom Gerety criticized those who burned the flag all the while defending their right to do so.[21] He chided the flag burners for not giving their names when asked who they were and for not engaging in discussion with those assembled to praise patriotism. His statement relied on an us/them rhetoric to separate the dissenters from others. "The flag burners at the rally," Gerety contended, "believed that America stands for evil and oppression. The rest of us believe not that America is perfect or without blemish—but above all that it is free." Gerety continued, "Most of us would probably not engage in the type of behavior demonstrated by the flag burners. . . . What these young flag burners did . . . hurt deeply many of us who feel with great immediacy and emotions the losses of September 11th."

But despite his condemnation and depiction of the flag burners as savage outsiders to "our" civilized community, Gerety deployed the language of rights to proclaim:

> As difficult as it is, this means that we have to respect the rights of all to speak freely, even insultingly, about our country, its principles and policies. "If there is any principle of the Constitution that more imperatively calls for attachment than any other," Justice Holmes wrote in a dissent in 1929, "it is the principle of free thought—not free thought for those who agree with us but freedom for the thought that we hate."

In dangerous times even such rights-based toleration may evaporate. In such times those in power—people like Ashcroft and Fleischer—assert that our way of life is at stake and treat the critic as an enemy.[22] In so doing they raise dramatically the always substantial price of dissent. They invite accusations of disloyalty and/or treason.[23]

DISSENT IN TIMES OF TERROR

And these are certainly dangerous times. Since the tragic events of September 11, 2001, the imagining of America has deeply changed. No longer do Americans live with a comforting sense of invulnerability; no longer can we live with the belief that great power guarantees national security.[24] Since September 11 we have been regularly reminded that terrorism collapses all boundaries; no place, no person lives away from the danger zone.[25] In the eyes of the terrorist we are all combatants.[26] War and toleration of dissent ordinarily do not easily coexist,[27] and if terrorism marks a condition of permanent war its consequences for dissent will surely be substantial.[28]

The shock and horror of September 11 shook the foundations of American complacency, reminding us of the underside of a global community divided by fundamental religious and political differences and deep socioeconomic disparities.[29] September 11 plunged America into a time of danger seemingly unprecedented in modern times. Yet, as in all times of danger, one part of America's response hardly seems unprecedented, namely, our national impatience with, and intolerance of, dissent.[30]

In times of war and stress, as the columnist Anthony Lewis puts it, "we have yielded again and again to fear."[31] Fear of the Jacobin terror in France fueled passage of the Sedition Act in 1798.[32] During World War I, men and women were sentenced to long prison terms for even mildly critical political speech.[33] In World War II, unreasoning fear led to the internment of Japanese Americans.[34] The Cold War fear of the Red Menace produced the abuses of McCarthyism.[35] Vietnam War protests were met with a substantial growth in domestic intelligence gathering designed to monitor and chill dissent.[36]

Since September 11 "fear again threatens reason."[37] Aliens have been imprisoned for months on the flimsiest of grounds.[38] The attorney general of the United States moved to deport people on the basis of secret evidence.[39] The president authorized military tribunals to hold trials under special rules,[40] and Congress passed the so-called USA Patriot Act.[41] National Security Advisor Condoleezza Rice requested that American television networks not air unedited broadcasts of statements by Osama bin Laden lest such statements might be encoded with messages intended for terrorists in the United States.[42] The American Council of Trustees and Alumni, a conservative academic group founded by Lynne Cheney, issued an indictment of more than forty college and university professors for post–September 11 statements that the council branded "short on patriotism and long on self-flagellation."[43]

Our leaders proclaim that unprecedented threats generate unprecedented responses.[44] Yet, for all of the sense that terrorism marks something radically new in American life, what is remarkable is that old, familiar arguments are unearthed, dusted off, fitted to the new circumstances of a seemingly more dangerous world, and used to justify assaults on civil liberties and civil rights.[45] Security seems again to trump dissent; once more it is offered up as the foundation of all our liberties and used to justify new policies that impose substantial costs on civil liberties.[46]

Commentators compare the post–September 11 war on terror to the Cold War's hysterical anticommunism.[47] Is ours a new McCarthyism? Or is it something different? While civil liberties seem more secure, more rooted in the practices of civil society, than they were fifty years ago, there is also a new spirit of intolerance in the community.[48] It is an intolerance that presents itself as patriotism and insists that dissent in dangerous times is incompatible with patriotism.[49] Thus in the immediate aftermath of September 11, flying the flag became a signal of belonging.[50] With flags everywhere, dissent seemed stifled, foreclosed, deprived of its in-betweenness, precluded before it could be articulated. In that situation censorship was the work of our fellow citizens. This kind of censorship was "more widespread and more effective" than the restrictions subsequently imposed by the government.[51]

One central element in this chilling of dissent has been the tidal wave of public opinion supporting the broad goals of defeating terrorists and protecting against terrorism.[52] Moreover, the Bush administration has used that mandate to convey the message that dissent is, if not downright un-American, at least very dangerous. Appearing before the Senate Judiciary Committee in early December, John Ashcroft said that domestic critics of U.S. policy "aid terrorists" and "give ammunition to America's enemies."[53] The news media and entertainment industry too to have been wary, too concerned about public reaction to give voice to anything other than mainstream views. Thus newspaper staffers at the *Texas City Sun* and the *Daily Courier* of Oregon were fired after writing columns critical of President Bush after September 11.[54] And the media learned a painful lesson when Bill Maher said on *Politically Incorrect* that lobbying missiles at targets from long distances would be "cowardly." The response was a firestorm in the face of which Maher issued a tortured apology.[55]

One result of these developments is that loyalty, if not patriotism, is today a force field within which dissent seemingly must operate if it is to be legitimate.[56] There is a deep anxiety, deeper than the usual worry that accompanies protest, that now attaches to acts of dissent. Dissenters, knowing of their vulnerability to charges of disloyalty, respond to this anxiety by insisting, ever more stridently, that dissent constitutes the truest expression of loyalty.[57] "Loyalty," Commager once insisted, "is devotion to the best interests of the commonwealth, and may require hostility to the particular policies which the government pursues . . . the particular institutions which society maintains. . . . It is a realization that America was born of revolt, flourished on dissent, became great through experimentation."[58] Instead of occupying a space of in-betweenness, dissent is fully inscribed within a national/nationalist narrative.[59] However, the relationship between dissent and loyalty is surely much more complex and vexed than these simple assertions—that dissenters are the true loyalists, the truest patriots, that America is the home of a vibrant dissident tradition—would have us believe.

OVERVIEW

The essays that follow, each in its own way, seek to complicate this picture of dissent in dangerous times. They do so by exploring the claims of belonging that animate acts of dissent, and they make critical and normative arguments about the psychic life of dissent. They describe the ways our political, legal, and cultural institutions portray dissent, and they explore the practices of the self that foster dissent and that dissent fosters. While this book is divided into two parts—"Citizenship, Dissent, and the Experience of Belonging" and "Responses to Danger in State and Society: Containing Dissent"—each of the essays recalls earlier eras and how they responded to danger, theorizes about danger and dissent as cultural, political, and legal phenomena, and examines the nature of political repression in liberal societies and the political and legal implications of fear. They all call on their readers to think about, and beyond, September 11, even as they warn of the danger to dissent in our dangerous times.

The first part contains two essays, one by Wendy Brown, the other by Lauren Berlant. Both take as their central concern the nature and price of political belonging in the world before and after September 11. Brown starts our inquiry by using sources from Socrates to Freud as theoretical lenses to explore the meaning of love, loyalty, and dissent. Starting from a post–September 11 world in which dissenters fear for their moral and political standing as Americans, Brown claims that "patriots" and dissenters are in fact united by a shared tendency toward what she calls "idealization." The patriot loves an idealized version of the nation, while the dissenter is moved by an idealized version of a world of yet-to-bes; the patriot idealizes *this* America; the dissenter loves *another* America against which he measures the acts of its present-day instantiation.

This kind of idealization, Brown claims, also characterized Socrates' idea of Athens. For him the best Athenian citizen was the critic whose dissent helped prevent an all-too-easy slide from thoughtlessness to injustice. Thoughtless conformity to convention was, for Socrates, the gravest danger of citizenship and the greatest temptation of belonging in a political community. In contrast, the Socratic dissenter honors the integrity of the collectivity through his intellectual labors and insists on examination of the taken-for-granteds that seem to be the glue of political community. He is devoted to the cultivation of virtue in himself, his fellow citizens, and their shared political community.

But Socratic dissent, whatever its original motives or its roots, is threatening to patriotism because it has the potential to incite a "generalized desublimation" of the repressed hostility that Brown, drawing on Freud, claims is always latent in extreme idealization of the nation. Patriotism elides, represses, this hostility, insisting that true loyalty can have only one mind, one disposition toward its object. In dangerous times, insistence on this single-mindedness, a single-mindedness that the Socratic critic sees as an excuse for thoughtlessness, intensifies. Collective idealization must, in these times, be internally policed for any signs of doubt, lest patriotism start to unravel. The dissenter resists this policing by refusing thoughtlessness and insisting that citizenship serves the political community through a continuous questioning of its progress toward virtue.

Socratic belonging, the belonging of the dissenter moved by reason and moved to serve reason, is according to Lauren Berlant in great danger in the political culture of contemporary capitalist democracy. One marker of our distance from the Socratic understanding is found in the critique of nuance that has marked the administration of President George W. Bush from its beginning. Well before September 11, but growing more intense after, the president and others have campaigned against nuance and linked the critical intellectual energy of dissent to a kind of civic amoralism.[60] They have used the political sphere for "the orchestration of public feeling."[61] They have moved the marker of citizenship and belonging from rational criticism to what Berlant calls "the visceral performance of moral clarity" and, in so doing, acted to collapse the in-between space that dissent seeks to occupy.

The post–September 11 intolerance for dissent grows out of the political culture of "true feeling" that Berlant has explored in some of her other work.[62] In this political culture emotional transparency is a vehicle for establishing national belonging, and what citizens share is pain.[63] The contemporary mass media celebrates what Berlant calls "emotional humanism" through its preoccupation with scenes of intense emotion, which contributes to a condition in which all pain, no matter what its cause, is treated as a marker of injustice.

Thus it is not surprising that the Bush administration's "War on Terror" is a war on feeling, or a particular kind of feeling, the intense fear generated by a perceived loss of the reassuring orderliness of boundaries, hierarchy, law. It is the shapelessness of the enemy within that sparks the greatest fear. Dissenters complicate the project of repairing these feelings by, like Socrates, carrying on a crusade against moral reductionism.

In making this argument, Berlant draws parallels between anticommunism and antiterror. Both depend on a series of ideological clichés in which the right to dissent is elevated while the practices of dissenters are condemned. Not surprisingly, the objects of critique in the campaign against terror, as in the campaign against communism, are centers of "counterhegemonic negativity"—the news media and universities.

In our contemporary conditions of danger we respond to our fears, Berlant argues, through practices of enumeration. We count what we have and what we have lost; we compulsively name the living and the dead. In so doing the national present is constituted as a "continuous site of urgency." Its urgency is unrelenting, leaving no space for anything but shared sentiments. We end up lavishing praise on the rather ordinary acts of capitalist reproduction, investing, consuming, and so forth, as if they were themselves a heroic response to current conditions of danger. In these acts we express a flattened kind of citizenship, while insistence on reasoned analysis of the sources of danger and dissent from policies that bring it about is marked as a special kind of disloyalty.

The next part of the book—"Responses to Danger in State and Society: Containing Dissent"—takes up this marking of dissent in a dangerous time in the responses of the institutions of state and society. Hugh Gusterson begins this part by considering the efforts of the American Council of Trustees and Alumni (ACTA), a conservative group founded by Lynne Cheney "to blacklist critical voices on campus after September 11." He locates that effort in the context of what he calls America's "tradition of repressing dissent in times of crisis," in particular, McCarthyism. Like Berlant, Gusterson sees continuities between

McCarthyism and our current situation, though in the end he argues that there are as many differences as similarities, differences that point to the "evolving nature of public discourse on state security and intellectual dissent."

In the 1940s and 1950s the state sought to colonize universities, long thought of as centers of opposition, by increasing funding for military research and, at the same time, enlisting them to blacklist dissident faculty members (as Berlant notes). University administrators, trustees, faculty, and outside groups like the American Association of University Professors actively and energetically collaborated in the effort to silence dissent by denouncing and punishing dissenters. So pervasive was their complicity that, Gusterson observes, much of the dirty work of McCarthyism was done directly by universities.

Today universities are again under suspicion, regarded as dangerous sites of cultural and ideological instability. However, their response to the ACTA blacklist was, Gusterson notes, much different than their previous complicity with McCarthyism. University administrators and trustees remained silent rather than joining the denunciation, and many faculty rallied to those who had been singled out by ACTA for making politically incorrect comments. In addition, outside groups and the media actively condemned ACTA and defended the right of its targets to dissent.

All of this would seem to indicate that today the right to dissent is safer than it was fifty years ago, at least in universities. Yet, despite seemingly greater tolerance for dissent in the war on terror than in the earlier anticommunist period, there is little evidence that the channels of effective communication are any more open to those who critique government policy today than they were fifty years ago. The result, Gusterson warns, is that dissent helps to legitimate American values without having any real chance of influencing policy. "Dissent," Gusterson concludes, is an "ornament of hegemony" and a weapon in the arsenal of American exceptionalism.

David Cole also uses the comparison to McCarthyism as a vantage point from which to examine responses to dissent in the post–September 11 world. He notes:

> As we launch a war on terrorism . . . , scholars, government officials, and pundits remind us repeatedly that we have avoided the mistakes of the past: we have not locked people up for merely speaking out against the

> war, as we did during World War I; we have not interned people based solely on their racial identity, as we did during World War II; and we have not punished people for membership in proscribed groups, as we did during the Cold War.

Yet, like Gusterson, he cautions readers against the easy conclusion that repression of dissent and difference is a thing of the past.

Cole argues that in the war on terrorism the government has substituted "new forms of political repression for old ones." It has shown considerable inventiveness in devising new mechanisms and new tactics to police and punish dissent, including the use of administrative procedures to detain more than 2,000 people largely because of their ethnic identity, subjecting noncitizens of Muslim and Arab origin to discriminatory deportation and surveillance, and making "guilt by association a linchpin of the war's strategy." Comparing McCarthyism to the war on terror reveals "not so much a *repudiation* as an *evolution* of political repression."

Cole concentrates on two tactics of the war on terror. The first involves a substantive expansion of the terms of criminal responsibility, the second the use of administrative processes to punish dissenters. The key example of the former is the enactment of legislation making it a federal offense to provide "material support" to terrorist organizations. This legislation does not require proof that an individual so accused intended to further terrorist activity. It is a crime merely to provide anything of value to a designated terrorist organization. "The 'material support' law," Cole argues, "is a classic instance of guilt by association" and enables the government to deter and, if not deter, punish wholly innocent political activity.

Cole's second example involves the use of administrative rather than criminal procedures to process persons the government deems threatening or subversive. Echoing the tactics of the Palmer Raids of 1919–20, the government has bypassed the criminal process through the use of immigration proceedings, the indefinite detention of citizens and foreign nationals as "enemy combatants," and administrative embargoes on the assets of suspect groups. Each of these devices can be used without having to prove "that any criminal activity was performed, planned, or even contemplated"; each has the effect of preventing those subject to them from invoking rights that would be available to them if accused of crimes. These devices, substantive and procedural, subvert some of the very principles—freedom of association, freedom of speech, no group guilt—that Cole asserts "distinguish us from the terrorists," and, in so doing, we are in danger of forfeiting "much of the legitimacy of the war on terrorism."

The last chapter of this book presents a theoretical perspective on the way governments, including our own, respond to conditions of emergency. It examines the psychic economy at work in those responses. In so doing it both broadens the analysis provided in the Gusterson and Cole chapters and returns to issues raised by Brown and Berlant about the psychic life of repression and dissent. Nancy Rosenblum's essay does this by discussing the idea of "reason of state," which, she says, "refers to the measures required for political survival—the deep necessities."

Reason of state appears in different forms depending on the nature of the political regime in which it is embedded. Rosenblum examines three examples in order "to point up the 'exceptionalism' of American constitutionalism in grappling with the demands of reason of state." Turning first to Machiavelli's discussion of dictatorship in the Roman Republic, "power was given to one man to make decisions without consultation and to execute them without appeal." This man was a constitutional dictator, not a tyrant, because he could not assume authority "on his own authority." From Machiavelli Rosenblum next turns to Locke. Locke conceded that there are situations that the law can not anticipate and responses that the law cannot prescribe. As a result, times of emergency call for "prerogative power," discretion exercised by the executive outside and against the law. For Locke the only guarantee against the abuse of prerogative is majoritarian opposition.

In contrast to the Roman Republic or Lockean constitutionalism, the American constitutional tradition insists on the "continuity between dangerous times, including wartime, and presumably peaceful normal times." Reason of state is fully inscribed, or so that tradition would have us believe, in the Constitution, which prescribes "what is permissible during emergencies as well as business-as-usual." The adequacy of this understanding of reason of state is, Rosenblum contends, before us as never before, as the state confronts terrorists who "took advantage of American openness" and dissenters who insist on "civil liberties absolutism or constitutional business-as-usual."

However, the fate of dissent in dangerous times, Rosenblum argues, involves more than the institutional arrangements that enable and constrain reason of state. It depends on the way government officials understand the new world we have entered. In dangerous times like these the worthiness of the existing political order provides the ground norm for action, "making its preservation the responsibility of governors." Just as dissenters act through a moral and moralized lens, so do those who would limit dissent in the name of national survival.

In dangerous times governors accept the responsibility for measures that they know "violate . . . the moral norms and legal rules that ordinarily constrain political action." Yet it is also the case that political authorities may exaggerate or exploit danger to justify exercises of power, including the repression of dissent, that might not otherwise be tolerated.[64] Like Brown's analysis of the psychic life of dissent, Rosenblum argues that those who seek to repress it bring to their opposition mixed motives, some noble, some base.

Rosenblum concludes her chapter by arguing that we cannot understand the response of the state to dissent in dangerous times if we concentrate exclusively on what she calls the "fear factor." Another positive emotion that animates that response is "the thrill of intense emergency energy and direct action." Emergency provides an opportunity for "revivification. It is an opportunity to put an end to ordinariness" or, as Berlant argues, to redefine the ordinary. Reason of state, necessity, emergency, each provides an "electric jolt" for those who govern, a chance to escape the drag of institutional checks and deliberative processes, to experience "the exhilaration that accompanies aggressive action." The energy that pours into repression fuels the adaptive inventiveness about which Cole writes and propels an "excited identification of political society with surveillance, force, and punishment." In the end, Rosenblum's analysis invites us to consider how far we have come from the political world that Socrates inhabited.

Taken together the essays in this book highlight the complexity of the dynamic of dissent and repression in dangerous times by reminding us of points of contrast between the loyalist's politics of feeling and the dissenter's insistent rationalism, as well as the extreme idealization that may animate both. They call us to reconsider the continuities and discontinuities that have marked America's historical responses to dissent in dangerous times. Should ours be a narrative of progress in the struggle to respect the space of dissent in times when national survival seems to be at stake or one of insidious adaptation and inventiveness by the forces of repression in state and society? The essays in this book help to reimagine the psychic economy of dissent and of responses to it, paying attention to the complex combination of hostility and attachment and of fear and pleasure that characterize both dissenters and those who seek to limit dissent. In all of this they enable us to confront the post–September 11 world of danger with new understandings and an awareness of new possibilities.

NOTES

1. Henry Louis Gates Jr., "Patriotism," *Nation,* July 15/22, 1991, 91. Shiffrin makes a similar point when he argues that "the dissent model would hope that dialogue would ultimately be spurred by the presence of dissent." Steven Shiffrin, *Dissent, Injustice, and the Meanings of America* (Princeton: Princeton University Press, 1999), 17. Also Wendy Kaminer, "Patriotic Dissent," 12 *American Prospect* (2001), 32.

2. For a discussion of this tension, see Charles Euchner, *Extraordinary Politics: How Protest and Dissent Are Changing American Democracy* (Boulder: Westview Press, 1996).

3. See *Abrams v. United States,* 250 U.S. 616, 630 (1919) (Holmes, J., dissenting). See also Henry Schofield, "Freedom of the Press in the United States," in *Essays on Constitutional Law and Equity* (1914), 11. "Men," Schofield wrote, "will be fined and imprisoned, under the guise of being punished for their bad motives, or bad intent and ends, simply because the powers that be do not agree with their opinions." As Shiffrin puts it, "Persons in power also have the all-too-human tendency to believe in good faith that the 'right' answers to moral and political issues just happen to be ones that consolidate and enhance their own power." Shiffrin, *Dissent, Injustice,* 92.

4. *Younger v. Harris,* 401 U.S. 37, 65 (1971) (Douglas, J., dissenting).

5. See Jeb Rubenfeld, "The First Amendment's Purpose," 53 *Stanford Law Review* (2001), 767, 782. "The right to engage in political dissent must surely yield when compelling governmental interests are implicated."

6. Shiffrin, *Dissent, Injustice,* xi.

7. See, for example, David Bromwich, "Lincoln and Whitman as Representative Americans," 90 *Yale Review* (2002), 1–21. On the ways in which this proposition is contested see James Davidson Hunter, *Culture Wars: The Struggle to Define America* (New York: Basic Books, 1991).

8. Henry Steele Commager, *Freedom, Loyalty, Dissent* (New York: Oxford University Press, 1954), 39. See also Abe Fortas, *Concerning Dissent and Civil Disobedience* (New York: New American Library, 1968), 24.

9. See, for example, Henry Canby, *Thoreau* (Boston: Beacon Press, 1958),

and Robert Dickens, *Thoreau: The Complete Individualist* (New York: Exposition Press, 1974).

10. See Erik Erikson, *Gandhi's Truth: On the Origins of Militant Nonviolence* (New York: Norton, 1969); see also Kenneth Keniston, *Young Radical's Notes on Committed Youth* (New York: Harcourt, Brace, 1968), and Kenneth Keniston, *Youth and Dissent: The Rise of a New Opposition* (New York: Harcourt, Brace, 1971).

11. Michael Kammen, "The Problem of American Exceptionalism: A Reconsideration," 45 *American Quarterly* (1993), 1. "America," Shiffrin contends, "has had a romance with the First Amendment." Steven Shiffrin, *The First Amendment, Democracy, and Romance* (Cambridge: Harvard University Press, 1990), 5.

12. George Kateb, *The Inner Ocean: Individualism and Democratic Culture* (Ithaca: Cornell University Press, 1992).

13. Id., 89, 90.

14. Shiffrin, *Dissent, Injustice,* xii.

15. Id., chap. 4.

16. Judith Butler, "Explanation and Exoneration, or What We Can Hear," 5 *Theory and Event* (2002), http://muse.jhu.edu/journals/theory_and_event/v005/5.4butler.html.

17. Judith Koffler and Bennett Gershman, "The New Seditious Libel," 69 *Cornell Law Review* (1984), 858. See also Michael Vitello, "The Nuremberg Files: Testing the Outer Limits of the First Amendment," 61 *Ohio State Law Journal* (2000), 1175.

18. Susan Ross, "An Apologia to Radical Dissent and a Supreme Court Test to Protect It," 7 *Communication Law and Policy* (2002), 401, 402. See also Zechariah Chafee, *Free Speech in the United States,* 2d ed. (Cambridge: Harvard University Press, 1942).

19. Shiffrin, *Dissent, Injustice,* 27.

20. See David Heyd, ed., *Toleration: An Elusive Virtue* (Princeton: Princeton University Press, 1996). Also Susan Mendus, *Toleration and the Limits of Liberalism* (Atlantic Highlands, NJ: Humanities Press International, 1989). Shiffrin argues that given the danger of dissent, "it is not enough to tolerate dissent; dissent needs to be institutionally encouraged." *Dissent, Injustice,* xiii.

21. http://www.amherst.edu/~pubaff/news/president/flagburning.html. For a similar argument see Justice Kennedy's concurring opinion in *Texas v. Johnson,* 491 U.S. 397 (1989).

22. Richard Johnson, "Defending Ways of Life: The (Anti-)Terrorist Rhetorics of Bush and Blair," 19 *Theory, Culture, and Society,* 211.

23. "Both the left and the right have confused dissent and treason: the McCarthyites of the 1950s often labeled dissenters as traitors, while the left often defended Soviet agents as mere dissenters." See Cathy Young, "Patriotism in Academia," *Boston Globe,* June 10, 2002, A15. Also Richard Reeves, "There is a Difference between Dissent and Treason," *Tulsa World,* December 15, 2001, Opinion, and Michael Brown, "There is Nothing Treacherous about Voicing Dissent at This Difficult Time," *Independent* (London), September 28, 2001, 4.

24. See Fred DallMayr, "Lessons of September 11," 19 *Theory, Culture, and Society* (2002), 137.

25. Agnes Heller, "Modernity and Terror," 9 *Constellations* (2002), 53.

26. Michael Ignatieff, "Terrorism and Human Rights," manuscript, 2002. Peter Hahn, "9/11 and the American Way of Life: The Impact of 12/7 Revisited," 26 *Diplomatic History* (2002), 627. Also John Millbank, "Sovereignty, Empire, Capital, and Terror," 101 *South Atlantic Quarterly* (2002), 305.

27. Zechariah Chafee, "Freedom of Speech in War Time," 32 *Harvard Law Review* (1919), 932. Also Koffler and Gershman, "The New Seditious Libel," 816.

28. See Robert Kuttner, "Terrorism and Our Democracy," *American Prospect*, September 21, 2001, www.prospect.org/webfeatures/2001/09/kuttner; Celestine Bohlen, "In the New War on Terrorism, Words Are Weapons Too," *New York Times*, September 29, 2001, A11.

29. Samuel Huntington, *The Clash of Civilizations: Remaking the World Order* (New York: Touchstone, 1996). For a different perspective on the same phenomena, see John Urry, "The Global Complexities of September 11th," *Theory, Culture, and Society* (2002), 57.

30. Sanford Levinson, "What Is the Constitution's Role in Wartime? Why Free Speech and Other Rights Are Not as Safe as You Might Think," *Writ*, October 17, 2001; http://writ.news.findlaw.com/commentary/20011017_levinson.html.

31. Anthony Lewis, "Hail and Farewell," *New York Times*, December 15, 2001, 31.

32. Marin Scordato and Paula Monopoli, "Free Speech Rationales after September 11th: The First Amendment in Post–World Trade Center America," 13 *Stanford Law and Policy Review* (2002), 185, 188.

33. Robert Murray, *Red Scare: A Study in National Hysteria, 1919–1920* (New York: McGraw Hill, 1955). Also Robert Warth, "The Palmer Raids," 48 *South Atlantic Quarterly* (1949), 1.

34. Peter Irons, *Justice at War* (New York: Oxford University Press, 1983).

35. For two different manifestations of the post–World War II attack on domestic communists see *Dennis v. United States*, 341 U.S. 494 (1951), and *Communist Party v. Subversive Activities Control Board*, 367 U.S. 1 (1961).

36. Richard Morgan, *Domestic Intelligence: Monitoring Dissent in America* (Austin: University of Texas Press, 1980), chap. 4.

37. Lewis, "Hail and Farewell."

38. David Cole, "Enemy Aliens," 54 *Stanford Law Review* (2002), 953.

39. William Glaberson, "U.S. Asks to Use Secret Evidence in Many Cases of Deportation," *New York Times*, December 9, 2001, 1B.

40. Matthew Purdy, "Bush's New Rules to Fight Terror Transform the Legal Landscape," *New York Times*, November 25, 2001, A1.

41. Jennifer Evans, "Hijacking Civil Liberties: The USA Patriot Act of 2001," 33 *Loyola University of Chicago Law Journal* (2002), 933. Also Emmanuel Gross, "The Influence of Terrorist Attacks on Human Rights in the United States: The Aftermath of September 11, 2001," 28 *North Carolina Journal of International Law and Commercial Regulation* (2002), 1.

42. The nature of Rice's request is described by Jason Zengerle, "Secrets and Lies," *New Republic,* October 30, 2001, www.thenewrepublic.com/express/zengerle103001.html. See also Gross, "The Influence of Terrorist Attacks on Human Rights in the United States," 80–81.

43. Patrick Healy, "Conservatives Denounce Dissent," *Boston Globe,* November 13, 2001, A7.

44. Johnson, "Defending Ways of Life." Also Ronald Dworkin, "The Threat to Patriotism," *New York Review of Books,* February 28, 2002, and Michael Glennon, "Terrorism and the Limits of Law," 26 *Wilson Quarterly* (2002), 12.

45. Kim Holmes and Edwin Meese, "Balancing Security and Liberty," *Heritage Foundation,* October 11, 2001, http://www.heritage.org/Press/Commentary/ed101101.cfm. Also Kim Holmes and Edwin Meese, "The Administration's Anti-Terrorism Package: Balancing Security and Liberty," *Heritage Foundation,* Backgrounder 1484, October 3, 2001. http://www.heritage.org/Research/NationalSecurity/BG1486.cfm. Valerie Demmer, "Civil Liberties and Homeland Security," 62 *Humanist* (January/February 2002), 7. Also Candace Cohn, "The Assault on Civil Liberties," 22 *International Socialist Review* (March/April 2002), http://www.isreview.org/issues/22/civil_liberties.

46. See Holmes and Meese, "Balancing Security and Liberty."

47. Examples are provided by Gusterson's and Cole's contributions to this book.

48. Richard Bernstein, "Counterpoint to Unity: Dissent," *New York Times,* October 6, 2001, A13. Also Jim Lobe, "The War on Dissent Widens," *Foreign Policy in Focus* (March 15, 2002), www.fpif.org/commentary/2002.

49. Kaminer, "Patriotic Dissent."

50. Joan Didion, "Fixed Opinions, or The Hinge of History," *New York Review of Books,* January 16, 2003, 54.

51. Commager, *Freedom, Loyalty, Dissent,* 75.

52. Mark Jurkowitz, "The Big Chill," *Boston Globe Magazine,* January 27, 2002, 11, 12.

53. Id., 18.

54. Billy Carter and Felicity Barringer, "In Patriotic Time, Dissent is Muted," *New York Times,* September 28, 2001, A1.

55. Jurkowitz, "The Big Chill," 21.

56. For an insightful discussion of the distinction between loyalty and patriotism, see George Fletcher, *Loyalty: An Essay on the Morality of Relationships* (New York: Oxford University Press, 1993), chap. 4.

57. "Patriotism does not oblige us to acquiesce in the destruction of liberty. Patriotism obliges us to question it, at least." Kaminer, "Patriotic Dissent," 32. See also Wendy Kaminer, "Fear Itself," *American Prospect,* December 3, 2001, and Thomas Platt, "The Concept of Responsible Dissent," 71 *Social Theory and Practice* (171), 41.

58. Commager, *Freedom, Loyalty, Dissent,* 146, 154. "Patriots," Richard Parker insists, "may as well criticize (even condemn) government as support it, in peacetime or wartime. What makes them patriots is that . . . they act in real and decisive measure out of potent personal attachment to their nation."

Parker, "Homeland: An Essay on Patriotism," 25 *Harvard Journal of Law and Public Policy* (2002), 407, 414.

59. Maurizio Viroli, *For Love of Country: An Essay on Patriotism and Nationalism* (Oxford: Clarendon Press, 1995).

60. See Johnson, "Defending Ways of Life."

61. "As if overnight," Didion contends, "the irreconcilable event had been made management, reduced to the sentimental, to protective talismans, totems, garlands of garlic, repeated pieties that would come to seem in some ways as destructive as the event itself." Didion, "Fixed Opinions," 54.

62. Lauren Berlant, *The Queen of America Goes to Washington City: Essays on Sex and Citizenship* (Durham: Duke University Press, 1997).

63. See also Jennifer Culbert, "The Sacred Name of Pain: The Role of Victim Impact Evidence in Death Penalty Sentencing Decisions," in Austin Sarat, ed., *Pain, Death, and the Law* (Ann Arbor: University of Michigan Press, 2001).

64. For a discussion of such tendencies in a different context, see Ryan Bishop and John Phillips, "Manufacturing Emergencies," 19 *Theory, Culture, and Society* (2002), 91.

Part I

CITIZENSHIP, DISSENT, & THE EXPERIENCE OF BELONGING

POLITICAL IDEALIZATION & ITS DISCONTENTS

Wendy Brown

> Ritual recognizes the potency of disorder.
>
> —Mary Douglas[1]

> Everything that the [love] object does and asks for is right and blameless . . .
>
> —Sigmund Freud[2]

What is political love and what is the relationship of political love and political loyalty? If one loves a political community, does such love require uncritical solidarity with certain elements of that community, and if so, with which elements—its laws, its principles, its state institutions, its leaders, or actions taken in its name? What kind of loyalty does political love engender and require? To what extent is love compatible with critique and to what extent is critique compatible with loyalty? What counterintuitive compatibility might be discerned between critique and fealty, between critique and attachment, even between critique and love?

This essay explores these questions about civic or political love, fealty, and critique through a consideration of the relationship of love and idealization. It considers this relationship as it emerges both in conservative expressions of national patriotism and in radical dissent from state policy. It asks about the productivity as well as the costs of political idealization and considers how we might successfully navigate some of its perils as we think about, and practice, democratic citizenship.

These reflections were incited by the widespread call for American national unity in the immediate aftermath of September 11. For the most part, this call demanded unwavering patriotism, uncritical support for state policy, and solidarity with a national narrative about our goodness and our victimhood. In this context, criticism of America or dissent from state policy were, quite simply, equated with disloyalty. And disloyalty, in turn, associated dissenters with what had overnight become the enemy.

The equation of dissent with disloyalty has its cultural and political ramifications, especially when combined with state declarations such as "if you're not with us, you're against us"—a formulation that tacitly endorses restrictions on dissent enacted by corporate and media powers while sustaining the legitimacy of the state as a protector of free speech.[3] However, the most worrisome ramifications may be less the explicit incidents of censorship than the discursive framing of all dissent as un-American, a framing that not only constrains what may be said *and* heard, but replaces a critically important political debate about what America is, stands for, or ought to do in world politics with a more polemical argument about loyalty or a more narrowly legalistic one about free speech. The instantiation of this polemicism and this legalism in the title and substance of the USA Patriot Acts, and in the now unquestionably necessary arguments about those pieces of legislation, is but one example of this diversion.

Two caveats before beginning. First, what follows is not a generic or universal formulation of the relationship between citizenship, loyalty, and critique; rather, it explores these relations as they are configured by a time of crisis and by a liberal democratic state response to that crisis. The essay does not ask, generically, whether there is some point at which political dissent or critique undercuts citizenship or some point at which political rebellion is legitimate. Rather, it considers the relation of love, loyalty, and critique within a political order, the existence and basic legitimacy of which is not called into question.[4] In other words, this is a distinctly nonrevolutionary formulation of the problematic of dissent; it not only presumes something of a stable nation-state population but presumes as well an investment from both critics and noncritics in preserving rather than overthrowing the state.

The second caveat concerns the effect on nation-state citizenship of the dramatic transnational migrations occasioned by the latest phase of capital, often termed globalization. My argument presumes reasonably strong identification by citizens with the nation-states in which they are living. However, this identification cannot be taken for granted today.

Western liberal democracies harbor substantial and growing populations that often have limited identification with and fealty toward the states they find themselves living in, or that may have fealty in the direction of two or more "nations," or that may assert a cosmopolitan "world citizenship" or "transnational citizenship" rather than one tied to a single nation-state. Apart from the question of immigration occasioned by globalization, nation-states themselves are receding, however slowly and unevenly, as the basis of collective identification and collective action. It may be that nothing is so important as trying to understand what nation-state citizenship—loyal, critical, disgruntled, or otherwise—means in this historical context, but that is not the aim of this essay.

1. SOCRATIC LOYALTY

We begin with Socrates and the complex model of radical patriotism that is figured in the Platonic dialogues concerned with his trial and death sentence. Socrates, who insisted on the intimacy of love and citizenship, love and knowledge, love and virtue. Socrates, who embodied a perverse but compelling form of citizenship rooted in challenging the premises and practices of the status quo, indeed, who made intellectual work into a distinct form of citizenship. Socrates, who would not flee the city that voted to execute him for his peculiar way of loving it but also would not be bullied into a more conventional form of affection. Surely this character is almost too extreme for thinking about today's dissident—only occasionally intellectual, often angry and alienated from other citizens, hardly a practitioner of love, and more likely to sue the state for abridged liberties than to bow before its sentencing. Yet, as the etymology of the word *theory* itself recalls—in ancient Greece, *theoria* emerged as a term for seeing enriched by journeying—there is often self-knowledge buried in places remote from our own.

In the *Apology* and the *Crito,* Socrates wrestles with the nature of his relationship and obligations to Athens, both of which configure his life as philosopher and critic, and both of which are activated as topics by his conviction and sentencing. Charged with corrupting the youth and with a specific kind of impiety—introducing new divinities—Socrates understands these charges to be rooted in the effects of his vocational calling and especially in the effects of his relentless critical interrogation of the contemporary Athenian way of life. In his defense against the charges, Socrates literally reverses them, casting his questioning of every individual and collective practice in Athens as loyalty not simply to an inner calling or to truth but to Athens itself. He roots this claim of loyalty in his love for the citizens of Athens, a love practiced and demonstrated by his commitment to improving them, a commitment for which he stakes his life. Pressing the argument still further, Socrates insists that he cares far more about Athenian citizens than his accusers do, indeed cares about them so much that he is willing to be put to death for his efforts on their behalf, just as devoted soldiers are willing to die in battle.

> For wherever a man's place is, whether the place which he has chosen or that in which [he] has been placed by a commander, there he ought to remain in the hour of danger, taking no account of death or of anything else in comparison with disgrace. . . . Strange, indeed, would be my conduct, O men of Athens, if I who, when I was ordered by the generals whom you chose to command me at Potidaea and Amphipolis and Delium, remained where they placed me, like any other man, facing death—if now, when, as I conceive and imagine, God orders me to fulfill the philosopher's mission of searching into myself and other men, I were to desert my post through fear of death. (*Apology* 28d–e)

The comparison with military service is no minor one, of course, since the soldier in battle is the ultimate icon of political loyalty, and it is Socrates' loyalty to Athens that is at issue. Yet the comparison could also not be more strained: the city's generals command the soldier while "God" commands Socrates, and the question of which god(s) Socrates hears or obeys animates one of the main questions about his potential civic subversiveness. Indeed, the tension between the fealty Socrates may have to a god other than Athens or to other than an Athenian god is articulated by this comparison even as it is also rhetorically finessed by it. If Socrates' daemon is uniquely his and if the god commanding him is Truth rather than an Athenian deity, then even his willingness to die for his commitment sustains rather than eradicates the potential tension between his inner calling and his civic loyalty, between serving truth and the effect of this service on the city he claims to love. Socrates finesses the tension through the trope of sacrifice and through the figure of the servant common to both, and thus allows obedience as such—to the point of risking death—to constitute proof of his loyal character. But civic patriotism is not loyalty as such and is not measured by willingness to die for one's cause whatever it is; rather it entails loyalty to the specific collectivity by which one is harbored and is generally measured by willingness to sacrifice for that collectivity.

Still, in this articulation and finesse, Socrates has articulated a dimension of our problem. Is political fealty appropriately attached to "actually existing political communities," to their laws, policies, or utterances, or to the political ideals we hold out for these communities? Is it sometimes one and sometimes the other? How do we know which, when? If one loves another Athens, another America than the one whose actions or laws one decries in the present, what is the place of loyalty in mediating between this love and the polity as it presents itself now, here? Or, if one loves what one is harbored by, but is also ruthlessly critical of and devoted to improving, is this loyalty? When might thoughtful disagreement or passionate critique be the ultimate act of love, even the ultimate act of solidarity—not simply because it is engaged but because it constitutes a more comprehensive address of this attachment insofar as it engages the ambivalence inherent in passionate attachment?

From Socrates in the *Apology*, we have an argument that dissent from existing practices, even wholesale critique of the regime, is not merely compatible with love and loyalty to a political community but, rather, is the supreme form of such love and loyalty. Moreover, it would seem that dissent can have this value even when it happens at the fringes of the regime, outside the domain of the officially political realm and thus outside the usual purview of citizenship, suggesting that it need not be a critique with immediate political efficacy (where the political is equated with policy). Socrates makes the case for intellectual critique as the highest form of loyalty if and when this critique is aimed at improving the *virtue* of the citizens.

In arguing that his unconventional ways and venue of working permit the greatest expression of political loyalty to the city, Socrates implies that the conventional political and military domains are not so fertile for the practice of loyalty understood as love—they are too fraught with immediate concerns of the day, with power politics, and above all, too inimical to the thoughtfulness that he takes as both the basis and the necessary content of this love; dutiful citizens carrying out an unjust policy or dutiful soldiers fighting an unjust war are presumably slavish and unthinking rather than loving in their loyalty.[5] What is also striking about Socrates' argument is that even as it is couched in terms compatible with modern Thoreauian themes of individual conscience, he is not making a moral or ethical argument but rather a political one about what constitutes true citizenship and loyalty. This is not simply a claim that "the examined life" is the most valuable thing for the polis. Rather, it is an argument that citizenship consists of a relation to individual virtue and justice, and is thus more importantly a relation of citizen to citizen than of citizen to state. Put starkly, Socrates defines good citizenship as the cultivation of virtue in oneself and others rather than in terms of an orientation toward law and the state.

Dana Villa's recent work, *Socratic Citizenship,* allows us to take this point further and to connect it with the problematic of critique. Villa argues that the Socratic activity of disputing common opinion—of what Villa calls "dissolving and purging"—would be mistakenly construed as only a project of disillusionment. Rather, drawing on Arendt, Villa argues that Socrates' commitment to thinking and to inciting thoughtfulness in his fellow citizens is a strategy for averting evil and injustice. In Arendt's study of Eichmann, she argued that the precondition for radical political evil is not some moral or ontological predisposition to evil but rather "ingrained thoughtlessness," and it is precisely such routine thoughtlessness that Socrates aims to disrupt.[6] If citizen virtue consists in avoiding evil, and if evil springs from such thoughtlessness, then thinking itself becomes the penultimate citizen virtue. Two conclusions follow from this positing of an inherent relation between thoughtfulness and justice and between justice and citizenship. First, any moral or political belief that is sheltered from interrogation, insofar as it becomes a thoughtlessly held belief, becomes an incitement to injustice.[7] Second, insofar as Socratic thoughtfulness—the work of interrogation and critique—requires a certain withdrawal from the immediate scene of political life, part of the action of political justice inherently occurs in a distinctly nonpolitical realm, in what Socrates called private life but in what we would call intellectual (not necessarily academic) life, a zone that is neither public nor private in the modern sense.[8]

In sum, Socrates' defense in the *Apology* would seem to make an argument for (1) critique as the basis for practicing virtue and justice, and hence as essential rather than inimical to civic loyalty;[9] (2) the space of this critique as one that either redefines the parameters of the political to include this intellectual work, this cultivation of thoughtfulness apart from the public realm or, alternatively, puts political life into necessary tension with intellectual life; (3) love of one's fellow citizens as the index of civic loyalty; and (4) devotion to improving citizen virtue as the index of this love. Again, this defense should not be misread as a valorization or cultivation of merely private virtue, merely individual dissent to the existing state, or merely intellectual critique of political life. Rather, Socrates aims to render politically potent a space (the private), an activity (philosophizing, critique), and relations (of individual citizens to one another and of the intellectual to the political) ordinarily conceived as unpolitical or irrelevant to the political. Perversely, his trial and punishment suggest at least partial success in this aim: the philosophical gadfly was figured by his accusers as a consequential political player in Athens.

But within the framework of political loyalty I have been developing via Socrates, what are the limits to critique? In particular, where might these limits obtain political definition? How far can critique go, and in particular how aggressive can it be toward the polity before it ceases to be loyal where loyalty is roughly equated with love? What must be preserved or protected amidst its deconstructive aims? The *Crito* offers something of an answer to these questions; the dialogue sketches a political container for the work of critique in the form of a warning against overly loosening the threads of the collectivity that sustain its inhabitants. Indeed, the dialogue as a whole represents a kind of limit on the activities defended in the *Apology*, a limit in which Socrates' own preference for living in the city of Athens is made to represent a tacit commitment not to violate or destroy the collectivity that has harbored, educated, and sustained him. The dialogue also contains an argument that the work of critique, Socrates' work, must be preservative, and to this end must be animated by love. Otherwise it will neither carry its own limits nor have any reason to be tolerated by those who wish to preserve the state. Socrates, in other words, was neither a simple defender of political free speech, nor a detractor of it. Rather, he crafts an argument about the *kind* of critical speech that is politically and ethically valuable and legitimate.

The dialogue begins with Socrates' corrupt old friend Crito coming to Socrates' prison on the morning he is to be executed with the aim of persuading Socrates to escape prison and flee Athens. Knowing it would be useless to ask Socrates to do this out of self-interest, Crito appeals to Socrates' sense of friendship: "People who do not know you and me will believe that I might have saved you if I had been willing to spend money, but that I did not care" (*Crito* 44c). This concern gives Socrates a final chance to respond to his accusers: he argues that the opinion of the many is unimportant compared to living virtuously, indeed that concern with the opinion of the many is at odds with living honorably (*Crito* 47–48). But then Socrates turns to the question of the proposed escape itself, asking not simply whether it would be acceptable to escape but whether it would serve virtue and justice to do so. For Socrates, this question ceases to be one concerned either with the character of his accusers or his alleged crimes and turns instead upon the nature of his belonging to Athens, and more specifically upon whether he may break the laws of Athens to preserve his own life.

Now, given Socrates' declared object of political attachment in the *Apology*, namely, the citizenry, why this sudden concern with the laws as an object and measure of political fealty? What force or authority are the laws being made to carry here? In the question of what constitutes his political obligation, why focus on laws rather than principles or practices—Socrates' usual focus in thinking about virtue? Why is an obligation to god, to truth, wisdom, philosophy, and virtue not more compelling than an obligation to the laws he has spent his life interrogating and criticizing, at times even belittling? And why this stubborn refusal to acknowledge that, in his own case, the laws have been, in Foucault's parlance, "used as tactics," and that in honoring the decision wrought from them, their tactical and corrupt deployment is dissimulated again?[10]

Why the laws? Socrates lets the laws themselves answer this question, which of course they do with great partiality to their case. They tell him first that the proposed act of escape is one that brings the state to ruin: "Do you imagine that a state can subsist and not be overthrown, in which the decisions of law have no power, but are set aside, and trampled upon by individuals?" (*Crito* 50b). They argue, second, that they are his true parents, "more precious and higher and holier by far than mother or father or any ancestor" and that as such, Socrates has no right to destroy them, even as they may have him destroyed (*Crito*

50e, 51a). So Socrates is enjoined from doing anything that ruins the state or that violates, degrades, or defies what has given him life, indeed, what has given him his lifework, what has made him Socrates. But is Socrates really arguing that the laws are the soul and sinew of the state? If so, what is the difference between disobeying the law (as he did, for example, when he refused to fetch Leon from Salamis) and refusing to submit to the law's punishment for disobeying it? Why is one kind of civil disobedience less harmful to the state than another? And what distinction does Socrates allow between the laws themselves and their interpretation and use by men? To which is one obliged? What is the significance, too, of this homage to the laws and the state from one who has just insisted upon the impossibility of knowing and pursuing virtue in public life, who has argued instead for the supervening value of tending individual souls—who has essentially argued against the potential for virtue in the political domain, a domain of which the laws are a part? Finally, in what sense are the laws "parents," and what is the significance of this discourse for thinking about Socratic dissent?

I want to suggest that *Crito* should not be treated as a literal defense of the laws as an object of unconditional fealty. Rather, read alongside the *Apology, Crito* argues for honoring, or better, *preserving,* whatever stands for the integrity of the collectivity, what binds and regenerates the collectivity over time. In the *Apology,* Socrates argued that intellectual life and especially its cultivation of thoughtfulness were utterly crucial in this regard. If the laws are also crucial, it is not because they are authoritative or because they are rules but because they generate and sustain the collectivity. When the laws say to Socrates, "we have brought you into the world and reared you and educated you," they are describing this generativity and posing the question of what it would mean to injure or demean it; they are reminding Socrates of his own constitution by the polis he has criticized, and they thereby delineate a crucial distinction between political critique and political destruction[11] (*Crito* 51c). Indeed, figured as parents, and speaking to him remonstratively, the laws recall the deep attachment—the love—that constitutes the ground and urgency of Socratic criticism; they configure such criticism as a force for improvement or transformation rather than destruction, and establish its limit at the place where the one veers into the other. The laws frame Socrates' work—they permit it (by permitting freedom of speech), they may well incite it (by being unjust or impoverished, or simply by provoking reflection about the justice they are meant to represent), but they also contain it as they contain him, indeed, as they *possess* him by virtue of their care for him.

There is another way to see this: the laws as Socrates has figured them in *Crito* are simultaneously dialogic and authoritative, intellectual and paternal. That is, on the one hand, they speak as Socrates ordinarily speaks, they become Socratic and interrogate Socrates as if he were one of the slightly dim-witted interlocutors he so often contends with, posing questions whose answers are largely given in the question and patiently leading Socrates to an inexorable and incontestable conclusion. But in assuming this dialogic character, they do not appear as static or formulaic things to be obeyed; rather they embody the very thoughtfulness and capacity for instruction and improvement that Socrates wants to place at the heart of the polis, that Socrates insists is the essence of justice. "All our orders," they declare, "are in the form of proposals, not of savage commands, and we give him the choice of either persuading us or doing what we say" (*Crito* 51e). In part, then, it is this dialogic and even philosophical quality of the laws that Socrates wants to protect and preserve. However, on the other hand, in the move to personify the laws as all-powerful parents—both generative of life and capable of taking it away—Socrates has also defined a locus of political authority that is not purely dialogic and certainly not a fount of freedom or egalitarianism. The laws describe Socrates as their "child and servant" and ask:

> Do you imagine that what is right for us is equally right for you, and that whatever we try to do to you, you are justified in retaliating? You did not have equality of rights with your father or your employer . . . ; you were not allowed to answer back when you were scolded or to hit back when you were beaten . . . Do you expect to have such licence against your country and its laws that if we try to put you to death in the belief that it is right to do so, you on your part will try your hardest to destroy your country and us its Laws in return? (*Crito* 50e).

So there is both authority and philosophical wisdom at the core of the laws' claim on Socrates, but in casting this combination in the figure of the father, Socrates has also gestured toward the idealization of the state so essential to its binding function as a state as well as generative of our loyalty to it. That is, in letting the authority of the laws stand for the state, in idealizing this authority as both powerful and wise (and yet also as vulnerable to injury), and in personifying this authority as parental, Socrates has recalled the libidinal and emotional investments that citizens must have in the insignias of the collectivity in order for the collectivity to bind a people together and command its fealty. At the same time, in personifying the laws as parents, Socrates has landed us on rich psychoanalytic terrain where parents are not just what one loves or reveres but also what one hates and wants to kill, what one desires either to have or to be, what one wants to triumph over or to destroy, what one wants to be loved by and for whose love one rivals one's siblings, what one has eternal longing, aggression, and guilt toward. Far from innocent, this metaphor calls out for closer consideration of the rich cauldron of affect toward the polity and the state that it signals.

2. FREUDIAN CIVIC BONDS

In taking up the challenge to think psychoanalytically about the state-citizen relation, we will not consider all that is entailed in formulating this relation in terms of the filial psyche but rather will focus upon the place of *idealization* and *identification* in generating political fealty and conditioning the specific problematic of dissent amidst this fealty. In particular, we will consider the ways that the extreme idealization of the state required for loyalty binds or suppresses an inherent hostility toward the idealized object, a hostility that dissent or critique may articulate. But not only articulate; rather, these isolated and episodic bouts of dissent or critique have the potential to incite a generalized desublimation of the repressed hostility in idealization—what Freud calls the "contagion effect" of violated taboos—thereby imperiling the consolidating power of the idealization. It is because it carries this potential that domestic dissent often appears and is cast (by the state, by patriotic citizens) as allied with attacks from outside—each exposes the vulnerability of the nation and what binds it, each de-idealizes albeit in a different way (one by challenging the good of the nation, the other by challenging its strength). The task, then, is to discern how critique can be fashioned as a productive de-idealization, one that features and preserves the love that incites or generates it. This challenge would require some reorientation on the part of both the critic/dissident and the patriot, the combined figure of which might be said to be Socrates, to whom we shall therefore eventually return.

From Freud, we learn that all love requires idealization and that idealization itself is a complex combination of narcissistic projection and sexual inhibition—the latter because love is already an inhibition of a more primary aim, sexual desire (*Group Psychology and the Analysis of the Ego,* 111–12). The mechanics of idealization are such that "the object is . . . treated in the same way as our own ego, so that when we are in love a considerable amount of narcissistic libido overflows on to the object" (112). In many cases, Freud argues, the love object is a substitute for some unattained ego ideal of our own—"We love it on account of the perfections which we have striven to reach for our own ego, and which we should now like to procure in this roundabout way as a means of satisfying our own narcissism" (113). For Freud, then, there is no such thing as simply loving an object for its intrinsically worthy qualities or capacities; the lover is always recasting the beloved according to her or his own ideals and ego needs. The lover is also always busily suppressing hostilities toward the love object in order to love *and* is always navigating between the desire to have and to be the love object. Idealization, which at its extreme refuses to countenance the perception of any flaws or limitations in the love object, assists in all of these projects, and this especially with love that is not sexually gratified. (Sexual gratification, Freud reminds us, inherently reduces the idealization or "overvaluation" that love entails—since love springs from repression of the sexual impulse.) Here is how Freud depicts this extreme idealization.

> Contemporaneously with this "devotion" of the ego to the object, which is no longer to be distinguished from a sublimated devotion to an abstract idea, the functions allotted to the ego ideal entirely cease to operate. The criticism exercised by that agency is silent; everything that the object does and asks for is right and blameless. Conscience has no application to anything that is done for the sake of the object; in the blindness of love remorselessness is carried to the pitch of crime. The whole situation can be completely summarized in a formula: *The object has been put in the place of the ego ideal.* (*Group Psychology,* 113)

Love is devotion to an abstract idea projected onto an object, but this devotion relieves the lover's superego of its ordinary tasks—that superego has been supplanted by the projections onto the love object. Thus, the lover is not only uncritically enthralled, without any capacity to judge or criticize the object, but also potentially criminal in this enthrallment—without any superegoic capacities of conscience to limit what he or she will do for the beloved or in the name of love. Although we are not quite ready to make the homological move to love of country, it is worth noting how this account resonates with a conventional kind of patriotic zeal. The patriot idealizes the country, which is indistinguishable from an abstract idea (e.g., of what America stands for) and devotes her- or himself to this ideal. The country is all, the patriot nothing, except in her or his devotion. There is no limit on what the country can ask for nor on what the patriot will do for the country, including violent, criminal, or suicidal acts.

To this point, we have considered idealization in love as an individual matter, but since we are trying to learn something about the ways of civic love, love that is oriented toward the state and embraces the collectivity that the state interpellates, we need to supplement this account with considerations of the dynamics peculiar to group idealizations. In *Totem and Taboo* and *Group Psychology and Analysis of the Ego,* Freud offers an analysis of the distinctive ways that love's complexities operate for groups and, more precisely, of how the reproduction of an ideal binds the group. In contrast with other moral and clinical psychologists of his day, Freud does not think that group and individual psychology stem from different parts of the psyche or involve different impulses; rather, for Freud, group psychology is an aspect of individual psychology, not a distinctive psychological form (*Group Psychology,* 69–70). This is so because Freud does not take human beings to be naturally solidaristic; to the contrary, we are inherently socially rivalrous and competitive, a feature born from sibling jealousies over parental love. Thus, Freud's challenge is to decipher what generates and then binds a group, which means tracking how individual psyches repress, divert, or sublimate this natural rivalry. Freud's answer is simultaneously simple and complex: group bonds are always based on shared love for something or someone that is outside the group and even at some distance from the group. "Originally rivals [individuals] . . . succeed . . . in identifying themselves with one another by means of a similar love for the same object" (120).

A group becomes possible, in short, when individuals put one and the same object in place of their ego ideal and consequently *identify themselves with one another in their ego.* Where for Hobbes, it is *fear* that gathers us, for Freud it is love; we are bound to one another through our collective experience of being in love with something that none of us can have, a bond that itself sustains the love and even gives the love a field of expression that the remoteness of the object would otherwise deny.[12] The group confirms the love and gives it a reality unavailable to the lone individual beholden to a remote object. (It is the sight of American flags everywhere, and not just his or her own, that gladdens the heart of the patriot.) In short, a group is achieved through identification in love, and is threatened by the sundering of that identification or the collapse of that love.

The difference between individual love and group formation, then, is that in the latter, individuals replace their natural rivalry toward one another with identification, an identification achieved by loving the same object. And when this love is not attached explicitly to a person ("a chief"), it will be to something else iconic of the group (e.g., the image of the nation, or the power of the nation), something outside that binds the inside. However, the attachment, given the nature of the displacement and identification it issues from, produces two very significant, indeed troubling effects for democratic citizenship even as it binds citizens into a nation: first, the attachment achieved through idealization is likely to glory in the *power* of the nation, a power expressed in state action; second, because individual ego ideals have been displaced onto the nation, citizenship and patriotism are rendered as relatively passive and uncritical adoration of this power. *Power thus replaces democracy as the love object, and passivity, obeisance, and uncritical fealty replaces active citizenship as the expression of love.* In this way, the psychoanalytic roots of nationalism appear as directly antidemocratic to the extent that democracy is understood as the sharing of power and the deliberation and thoughtfulness such sharing requires.

Moreover, this kind of love depends upon sustaining a very high level of idealization to counter the hostility that all feelings of love involve, and it depends as well upon externalizing this hostility. As Freud puts the matter in *Civilization and Its Discontents,* "it is always possible to bind together a considerable number of people in love, so long as there are other people left over to receive the manifestation of their aggressiveness."[13] The development of group cohesion thus depends upon turning aggression and hostility outward; maintenance of this cohesion depends upon keeping that aggression externalized; group narcissism allows the group to do this guiltlessly and even across potentially divisive stratifications within the group.[14] Still there is a precariousness to this achievement. First, in Freud's account, high levels of idealization, and particularly expressions of unqualified adoration and devotion, are themselves often signs of the unconscious hostility inherent in love. As he argues in *Totem and Taboo,* solicitous "over-affection," for example, of a young child for a mother, or between members of a married couple, is a way of "shouting down" this hostility and therefore also an obvious sign of its presence.[15] So the lover finds her- or himself in a condition in which she or he must refuse all evidence of flaws in its object, shout down its own aggression toward the object, and denounce others' aggression toward the object. This condition compounds the tendency, already identified in the psychodynamics of nationalism, toward a radical rejection of what we have identified as Socratic thoughtfulness, both in oneself and in others; indeed, this condition will necessarily equate thoughtfulness with potential danger to the idealization and hence to the polity. It is a condition that is inherently anti-intellectual. It is also a condition that would appear to entail lots of shouting.

The replacement of rivalry with identification through group love for the same object is precarious, second, because of what Freud formulates as anxiety about the contagion effect of taboo violation—a violation that breaks the collective awe of the taboo and especially the commitment to repressing hostility toward the revered object or being that is represented by the taboo. In Freud's account, the fear is that if one person succeeds in gratifying a repressed or unconscious desire, and that gratification is not immediately punished or avenged by the group, the same desire is bound to be kindled in other members of the community (*Totem and Taboo,* 71). To avert this contagion in the context of a relatively free social order, there must be a relatively even suppression of ambivalence toward the collective love object among members of a group. That is, the level of collective idealization must be pitched high and must be internally policed, even if this policing is not legally sanctioned or institutionally enforced. This is the basic structure of conventional patriotism's intolerance of critique.

We can now understand how sharp internal criticism of a nation, for those who have invested their uncritical love in it, does not simply entail the wound of having one's love object faulted but rather appears to threaten the very bonds of the nation by challenging both the identification and the idealization constituting these bonds. Moreover, such criticism effectively gives voice to the hostility suppressed by undying devotion, and once voiced, this hostility is potentially contagious, again threatening both the identification and the idealization that binds the nation. Finally, to the extent that such criticism does figure a certain unleashing of aggression toward the nation, it represents the desublimation of aggression in group love that is ordinarily turned outward toward what is named as an enemy. That is, if groups achieve harmony within by diverting aggression outward, not only toward that which does not share their love but toward that which is imagined as opposite to their love—figured as the Other of their idealized object—criticism brings the aggression back inside, which again threatens the identification as well as the idealization binding the nation.

This aggression turned inward, of course, can be turned again, by the patriots or the state, against the dissenter. Nothing does this more effectively than the discursive mechanism of linking domestic dissent with the enemy, correlating internal critique or de-idealization with external attack—"if you're not with us, you're against us." But this is not a purely tactical move. Both external attack and internal dissent wound the narcissism of the lover by challenging the idealization, especially if that idealization fetishizes strength or invulnerability and not simply goodness. Both threaten the group with disintegration; both reveal the thinness of the membrane binding the nation. It is hardly surprising, then, that they would appear not merely equivalent but collusive, leading the zealous patriot to denounce the dissenter as a traitor—"giving aid and comfort to the enemy."

Briefly now I want to make a turn from Freud to Žižek in order to plot one more line in this picture, one that will deepen our understanding of the peculiar character of identification involved in a certain kind of patriotism, and one that will allow us to see why dissent is not only problematic for maintaining idealization in general, but for maintaining the kind of identification upon which a liberal democratic patriotic ideal depends. In *The Sublime Object of Ideology,* Žižek theorizes political idealization as dependent not merely upon imaginary but also upon symbolic identification. Whereas imaginary identification is identification with the *objects in* an image, symbolic identification involves identification with the gaze that produces the image, and thus it is not only socially located elsewhere from the depicted objects but may be animated and organized by very different desires and social forces. In Žižek's own words, "Imaginary identification is identification with the image in which we appear likeable to ourselves, with the image representing 'what we would like to be,' and symbolic identification, identification with the very place *from where* we are being observed, *from where* we look at ourselves so that we appear to ourselves likeable, worthy of love."[16] So, for example, in an image of America as good, free, and true, but injured by evildoers who "hate our way of life," imaginary identification involves identifying with wounded goodness, while symbolic identification identifies with the power that generates this image, "the place from which such 'good' images are seen . . . the place of those who need to legitimize their domination and exploitation of others, those who disguise their aggressivity through the active invocation of a positive image that becomes . . . the symptom, the excess, the secret enjoyment of their lives."[17] If imaginary identification tends toward identification with powerlessness in such scenes, symbolic identification identifies with power but dissimulates this identification in the image of purity or woundedness through which it is achieved.

In her discussion of Žižek, Rey Chow notes that the significance of symbolic identification is often neglected (in intellectual and political life) precisely because it does not rely upon resemblance.[18] Thus, not just ordinary discourse but theoretical discourse tend to treat idealizations rather literally, that is, as a literal idealization of a loved object—whether an individual, a polity, a class or group—and fail to ask the questions "For whom is the subject enacting this role? Which gaze is considered when the subject identifies himself with a certain image?"[19] That is, even when citizens are identifying with images, say, of an innocent and well-meaning people, this imaginary identification is performed for an observing gaze, potentially internal but mirroring the external one of the powerful imperial state. The imaginary and symbolic identifications are thus made simultaneously and in relationship to one another.

The idealizations that symbolic identification generates and lives off of are extremely powerful as legitimation strategies; the work of symbolic identification here is to generate a patriotic ideal that disavows its imbrication with state violence, imperial arrogance, and aggression toward outsiders. In Rey Chow's account, the point of language that "proclaims/presents a noble idea/image of 'the people'" is "to seduce—to divert attention away from the rulers' violence and aggressivity at the same time that sympathy/empathy with the good idea/image is aroused."[20] The image of a free and good people conjured by contemporary patriotic idealizations generates sympathy, especially if such a people have suffered a wound, but this sympathy, indeed, this idealization, masks the symbolic identificatory function that it also generates—identification with the power that can generate such an image in the first place, that is outside the wound, that delivers the wound, that may be noninnocent, powerful, ignoble, imperial, and/or abusive.[21] Identification with power, which is what "my country is always right" patriotism entails, calls for loyalty to power rather than principle; it glories not in the goodness of America but in its power, and it needs other nations and peoples to defer to this power, indeed suffers a narcissistic wound when they do not.[22] This is a dangerous political condition, not only because of the volatility and aggression in this kind of patriotism but because it breeds anti-intellectualism, contempt for thoughtfulness and collective introspection, and disdain for peacemaking. Certainly the wrath turned against any attempt, in the autumn of 2001, to understand how America contributed to its own making as a target of third world and specifically Arab rage is a symptom of this condition. Indeed, the extent to which the plaintive and victimized refrain "Why do they hate us so?" was accompanied by a relentless refusal to entertain plausible answers to the question exemplifies the double operation of imaginary and symbolic identification in patriotic idealizations of America. The question invokes the image of aggression against our innocence and goodness and invites identification with the victimized innocents; the refusal identifies with the arrogance of state power and supremacy that feels no need to know anything about its place in the world or, indeed, to know much of anything about the rest of the world.

Žižek's distinction between imaginary and symbolic identification allows us to understand the extent to which a seemingly benign patriotic identification, one based in a celebration of the "American way of life," may disguise its own love of state power, its own enthrallment to the power of the father, indeed, its own potential feasting upon state violence. The patriotism formally features the goodness of the regime and the fineness of the people, not the power of the father to give or take away life, not what Socrates, in openly describing the paternal nature of the state and the filial nature of his obligation or fealty, expressed more directly—that it is in relation to the state's *power* that he curtails his defiance of the state and becomes deferential. This curtailment arises not from intimidation by state power but because he responds libidinally to this aspect of the state, because he idealizes the state as the father, and idealizes the father as a literally boundless object of devotion and love. This is the idealization that binds Socrates' own aggression toward the state (expressed in critique), the idealization that limits what he will do in the name of criticizing or attacking the state, the idealization that tempers his dissidence.

But since this idealization itself is a sign of love, we may also read Socrates as explicitly, perhaps even deliberately, working the ambivalence in love in such a way that the aggression has a productive field and is not only contoured by the attachment but made responsible by it, and put into its service. Recall that Socrates does not simply make a case for the importance of tolerating his philosophical critique of the polity but, rather, casts his work as the ultimate form of citizenship. Indeed, the very fact that Socrates affirms his fealty to the state through a philosophical inquiry into whether it would be just to escape his sentencing is a rhetorical demonstration of how his critical philosophical activity works in the service of his love of Athens. A citizen less committed to thoughtfulness might have fled, or cut a deal . . . as the patriotic scoundrels often do.

But if dissent is, potentially, a form of love, and if all love entails idealization, what might be the idealization entailed in relentless practices of dissent or critique? This is a question so complex that most of its provocation must be held for another essay. What can be acknowledged here is that idealization of an eternally deferred elsewhere, of a utopian version of one's polity, surely animates the work of the radical critic just as idealization of the existing state of things, or more often, of a polity's past, animates the conservative patriot. What is interesting about the figure of Socrates is that he harbors both kinds of idealization, and in rather extreme fashion. However, cultivating these two idealizations at the extreme is not the only way the tension between critique and fealty can be managed. The tension might be maintained such that one feels for the limits to critique in part by avowing the attachment that fuels it, by affirming the love, for example, of this America or of another America, animating the anger or disappointment. This is not to say that the attachment itself should be shielded from interrogation, but interrogating attachment and disavowing it are quite different matters.

If critique could be expressly tendered as an act of love, if it could be offered in a Socratic spirit, might it also be received differently? Perhaps it would appear less threatening to those who, consciously or unconsciously, experience it as assaulting their love object and as undermining the collectivity rallied around this love object. And if it were received differently, if it were not castigated as disloyal, un-American, or destructive—and thus placed outside legitimate political discourse—perhaps this would incite popular critique itself to more thoughtful, less moralistic or rebellious codes of conduct. It might then inhabit the dignified and authoritative voice of belonging, rather than the moral screech of exclusion. It might also be proffered in the voice of love and desire (for a better nation) rather than the voice of rage, shame, or denunciation. Conversely, if ambivalence in love could be forthrightly avowed in the formation of civic loyalty, the level of idealization (aimed at binding and shouting down this ambivalence) could be substantially lowered, and so also might the shouting be reduced. If loyalty did not seem to require this shouting-down of criticism, this refusal of thoughtfulness itself, then in turn the way might be opened for apprehending rich civic debate—even (perhaps especially) in times of crisis—as harboring the potential to strengthen rather than undermine a democracy.

Michael Ignatieff, also thinking through Freud about questions of civic belonging, draws from this thinking the conclusion that "we are only likely to love others more if we love ourselves a little less."[23] This view, I think, aptly characterizes the contemporary "cosmopolitan" antidote to problems thought to be posed by parochial attachments and fundamentalist passions, in short by nationalisms big and small. The larger, more worldly view, and hence the one to be counted on for peace, liberal civility, and tolerant coexistence, is considered to require a reduction of local zeals and loyalties, along with a corresponding increase in moral and political detachment. But this formulation remains trapped within the zero-sum Freudian economy in which "civilization" is enhanced or advanced only by depriving Eros of ever more gratification. I am suggesting a somewhat different route, one that brings reason and consciousness to practices of love rather than keeping them forever sequestered from one another, rather than asking reason to displace love on the one hand or barring love from reason and thoughtfulness on the other. This would involve developing political self-consciousness about the nature of civic love and developing as well certain practices to counter the potential destructiveness and antidemocratic energies and affects of such love. Specifically, it would require avowing the aggression and ambivalence in love, developing less dangerous outlets for the former and political lexicons that harbor the latter. It would require appreciation of the particular difficulties of group love and tracking the internal idealizations and external demonizations that arise to finesse these difficulties. And it would require reckoning with the lack of identity and unity in civic love over space and time so as to grasp how certain kinds of civic fervor arise to force oneness and permanence where it does not naturally inhere. Habits of political discourse that thematized these phenomena, or even simply monitored their effects, would not only reduce animosity toward dissent in times of crisis but help to reset dimensions of the typically imagined trade-off between national security and democracy, between a democratic polity's strength and the polyvocality that signifies democracy itself. Above all, such habits might cultivate the possibilities for a love of country oriented toward a thoughtful and empowered rather than passive citizenry, a love of democratic practices rather than nation-state power.

NOTES

1. *Purity and Danger* (New York: Praeger, 1966), 94.

2. *Group Psychology and the Analysis of the Ego,* in the *Standard Edition of the Complete Psychological Works of Sigmund Freud,* vol. 18, trans. and ed. James Strachey (London: Hogarth Press, 1961), 113.

3. For extended consideration of this point, see my forthcoming book, *Regulating Aversion: Tolerance in the Age of Identity and Empire,* especially chapter 4, "The Governmentality of Tolerance."

4. Precisely because of the limited scope of this essay's concern with dissent, it should not therefore be read as an endorsement of the Burkean injunction against challenging fundamental features of an established political collectivity or against calling for a fundamental transformation of the collectivity. One can legitimately argue, as an American, for a vision of America as a politi-

cally and economically decentralized, multicultural socialist democracy; just as one can argue, as an Israeli, for a vision of Israel as a democratic secular state. Of course there are those who would contend that these are no longer visions of America or Israel but rather constitute their abolition. Samuel Huntington, for example, has famously argued that "a multicultural America is impossible because a non-Western America is not American. . . . multiculturalism at home threatens the United States and the West" (*The Clash of Civilizations: Remaking of World Order* [New York: Simon and Schuster, 1996], 306). There is no way to settle the question of when critique is internal to the constitutive terms of a polity and when it is external, of when a particular vision extends the history of a nation and when it constitutes a rupture with that history.

5. Thus, Socrates explains why he could "not venture to come forward in public and advise the state" (*Apology* 31c), why, even when he was a senator, he went home rather than carry out a policy he considered illegal, and why he refused to carry out the orders of the oligarchy even as he risked death for doing so.

6. Dana Villa, *Socratic Citizenship* (Princeton: Princeton University Press, 2000), 22–23.

7. Ibid., 23.

8. Ibid., 6.

9. Foucault develops a notion of critique as virtue in his essay "What Is Critique?" See also the discussion by Judith Butler, "What Is Critique? An Essay on Foucault's Virtue." Both are in *The Political*, ed. David Ingram (Oxford: Blackwell, 2002).

10. Michel Foucault, "Governmentality," in *The Foucault Effect: Studies in Governmentality*, ed. Graham Burchell, Colin Gordon, and Peter Miller (Chicago: University of Chicago Press, 1991), 92.

11. At times, this distinction may be so fine as to be almost unsustainable. It does not turn upon a putative difference between words and actions. Nor does it turn upon the difference between questioning the laws and disobeying them; legal authority can be more radically undermined by the former than the latter. Rather, as I shall argue in what follows, I think it turns upon avowal of attachment to the object of critique and the limit this avowal may set on the destructive reach of the critique.

12. One of Freud's best examples here helps us understand not only political patriotic fervor but the phenomenon of thousands of screaming teenage girls clutching each other in shared delirium at a pop concert: "We have only to think of the troop of women and girls, all of them in love in an enthusiastically sentimental way, who crowd round a singer or pianist after his performance. It would certainly be easy for each of them to be jealous of the rest; but, in the face of their numbers and the consequent impossibility of their reaching the aim of their love, they renounce it, and instead of pulling out one another's hair, they act as a united group, do homage to the hero of the occasion with their common actions, and would probably be glad to have a share of *his* flowing locks." *Group Psychology*, 120.

13. *Civilization and Its Discontents,* in the *Standard Edition of the Complete Psychological Works,* vol. 21, 114.

14. In *Future of an Illusion,* Freud argues: "The narcissistic satisfaction provided by the cultural ideal is also among the forces which are successful in combating the hostility to culture within the cultural unit. This satisfaction can be shared in not only by the favoured classes, which enjoy the benefits of the culture, but also by the suppressed ones, since the right to despise the people outside it compensates them for the wrongs they suffer within their own unit. No doubt one is a wretched plebeian, harassed by debts and military service; but, to make up for it, one is a Roman citizen, one has one's share in the task of ruling other nations and dictating their laws." *Standard Edition of the Complete Psychological Works,* vol. 21, 13.

15. *Totem and Taboo,* trans. James Strachey (New York: Norton, 1950), 49.

16. Slavoj Žižek, *The Sublime Object of Ideology* (London: Verso, 1989), 105.

17. Rey Chow, *Ethics after Idealism: Theory-Culture-Ethnicity-Reading* (Bloomington: Indiana University Press, 1998), 42.

18. Ibid.

19. Žižek, *The Sublime Object,* 106.

20. Chow, *Ethics after Idealism,* 43.

21. Žižek's exploration of the hidden work of symbolic identification in legitimating a regime focuses on totalitarianism. However, for Žižek, totalitarianism is not opposed to the ordinary workings of ideology in modern Western states but rather is its strong version, or more precisely its cartoon version.

22. This would help interpret the self-described "pumped up" feeling some American men reported in the days after the World Trade Center attacks, incarnated not only in a desire to "get revenge" but also reported by Netscape as manifesting in an increased desire for sex and for red meat.

23. "Nationalism and Toleration," in Susan Mendus, *The Politics of Toleration: Tolerance and Intolerance in Modern Life* (Edinburgh: Edinburgh University Press, 1999), 81.

THE EPISTEMOLOGY OF STATE EMOTION

Lauren Berlant

Politics is the art of suppressing the political.[1]

—Jacques Rancière

I. A POLITICAL WEATHER REPORT

Nuance quickly became a moral buzzword of the George W. Bush administration: even to pursue nuanced thought was deemed a performance of antipatriotism. Linking dissent and amorality with a kind of pedantry that others might call critical intellectualism or just close reading, the ideologeme's radiant reign began in June 2001 with Peggy Noonan's "A Chat in the Oval Office," during which the president spoke in broad strokes about the significant post–Cold War potential opened up by Russia joining NATO, while acknowledging that "I haven't thought about the nuance of it." But the most noteworthy presidential usage came during an April interview on Britain's ITV. President Bush remarked

> Sure, people have—look, my job isn't to try to nuance. My job is to tell people what I think. And when I think there's an axis of evil, I say it. I think moral clarity is important, if you believe in freedom. And people can make all kinds of excuses, but there are some truths involved.[2]

Subsequent debates between Bush administration officials and those who disagreed with their policies were frequently phrased in terms of pro-Bush characterizations of nuance as something between pedantic nuisance and genuine treason. Meanwhile, the anti-Bush public responds to anti-nuance epistemology in kind, condemning the president's apparent incompetence at or refusal of reason in terms that range from charges of stupidity to antidemocratic, even fascist authoritarianism. Each side feels strongly that its way of knowing secures the relevant facts in support of political and moral right.

> *nuance:* French, from Middle French, shade of color, from *nuer* to make shades of color, from *nue* cloud, from Latin *nubes;* perhaps akin to Welsh *nudd* mist. Date: 1781[3]

II. VISCERAL POLITICS

Providing a context for debates about state power, economy, and community (thereby helping to shape the practices of the representative state) has been considered the main function of the public sphere.[4] This essay contests the notion and norm of political rationality as the core practice of democracy in the United States by considering the national political sphere not as a real or ideal scene of abstraction-oriented deliberation, but as a scene for the orchestration of *public feelings*—of the public's feelings, of feelings in public, of politics as a scene of emotional contestation.[5]

The import of this shift from the notion of a rational critical public to an affective public is both conceptual and historical, and does not deny the ongoing operation of cognition in the political sphere. While the political sphere is not void of rational thought, its dominant rhetorical style is to recruit the public to see political attachments as an amalgam of reflexive opinion and visceral or "gut" feeling (visceral, from the Latin *viscera,* intestine). The folding of thought into feeling modes of personal expressivity is not a sign of the decline of democracy or civil society per se, though. Feelings are not the opposite of thought: each is an embodied rhetorical register associated with specific practices, times, and spaces of appropriateness. Nor are feelings less abstract than thought: distinguishing these categories typically involves decisions about whether certain emotions conventionally associated with bodily reactivity have more or less value because of their seemingly expressive immediacy. Why should cognition seem more cultivated than emotion, since both are shaped by formal and informal pedagogies? My view is that this distinction is mainly normative: like emotion, cognition involves bodily responses, but while emotional expressivity is deemed spontaneous and hardwired, cognition's conventional modes of response escape notice except when they are admired as fine manifestations of self-control.[6]

This essay tells a story about the War on Terror currently pursued by the Bush administration in the aftermath of the Pentagon and World Trade Center attacks of 2001. What does it tell us about the political sphere that the government has deemed it a plausible strategy of consensus making to wage war not on terrorism or terrorists as such, but on Terror, a feeling, a feeling deemed evidence of injustice and justification for state antinomianism? The vague, shapeless, and pseudo-transparent qualities of Terror, and the relative autonomy of Terror from events and agents, make it possible for the government to motivate a situation of unending war and juridical crisis as though these practices constitute the just response of a representative state to the felt needs of its citizens.

The emotional tonalities of this administration are not unprecedented politically. The history of U.S. political modernity registers a shift of priority within normative, performative power styles from the rational circuit of opinionated argument to the visceral performance of moral clarity, which then may be supported by argument and evidence, but not of the sort traditionally taught involving hypotheses and ordered proof. I do not mean to argue, though, that sensationalism, hyperbole, and passionate irrationality are particular to the U.S. twentieth century, the political sphere, or the contemporary right wing. Absolutist and democratic, authoritarian and progressive regimes of power have long generated moral-hyperbolic dominant and oppositional rhetorical modes. But during the U.S. twentieth century, an emotional style linked to moral claims about truth and justice increasingly came to dominate ordinary political speech.

The following sections of this essay sort out some aspects of the place of emotional epistemology in the work of moralist politics in the U.S. political public sphere, moving among symptomatic cases—of the expressive performance style of World War II–era popular antifascism, the right-wing paranoid style of subsequent Cold War political performance, and the wielded presumptions of religious, affective, and moral clarity of the Republican right in the United States. In so doing I am charting a genealogy of right-wing antifederalist rhetorical affectivity, for I think the centrality of emotion to the claim to be viscerally and morally above politics goes far to explain the Bush administration's style of response to the crisis. I could also have focused on the affectivity of the anecdote in Ronald Reagan's rhetoric, or the space of derision and permission opened up by Bill Clinton's eloquent emotional openness to the suffering of others, were I trying only to make the broader case about the rise of moral-emotional rhetoric from a marginal to a dominant idiom of power. This essay moves toward understanding the current relationship between moral-affective publicness and the Bush administration's political practice.

We can pursue this development along technological lines as well. Mass culture theorists describe the centrality of the sense of "liveness" to the electronically mediated experience of national belonging, an affective experience of the world of events that comes to consumers as though immediate or made even more live and alive through the "you are there" qualities of radio, television, video, and film.[7] Liveness shapes the consumers of mass media into a public that has become such by encountering events marked by others as making the collective experience of now, "now" being a space- and time-making event deemed important as the present moment of a future history. This means that, insofar as the public is presumed to be identical with the polity, national publicness is a normative effect of communications that show to the public events that are already cast as constituting the collective experience of the national present. This is what Noam Chomsky, via Walter Lippmann, means by "manufactured consent."

Note the complex temporalities here: a subjective public experience of the present as a historical period is constituted by a preframing of events *x* as collectively significant at an observational metalevel, regardless of content. Not only is the political spectator deemed already to have consented to the priorities of the now hegemonic event, but she is also solicited to feel the impact that provides evidence that she belongs to the public constituted as a mass of spectators who see what she sees and feel what she feels, within a range of appropriate variation. Even more paradoxically, insofar as the citizen of liveness is moved rather than moving, the collective experience of social belonging privatizes her at the same time as it provides a subjective experience of participation in publicness.

How is this possible? Publicness is a zone of collective intimacy that does not require anyone meeting anyone else face to face: the very spatial abstractness of concepts like public and polity enable, theoretically, anyone's identification with and by them. Regardless of one's particular view about their own participation in the generalized public, subjects who live somewhere are connected to each other insofar as they recognize the performative force of formal law *and* the authority of informal customs of social projection. In this sense publicness requires individual recognition of the juridical constraints on individuality. At the same time, the mass-mediated scene of visceral engagement attaches personal to public experience and enables consuming subjects to have strong responses that seem to place them squarely in the emotional stream of collective life. The intensified impact of liveness can produce subjects who *feel* the life that is reported to be elsewhere without having to leave the home space. In this zone of privacy,[8] it is easy to imagine one's private consumption of particular events as scenes of genuine "public" trauma or joy: emotions can feel central to the national-popular domain without being especially political. Indeed, the emotional connection to other spectators also consuming history takes place at the same time that we see emerging a sense of privacy as personal political irrelevance and/or safety from the harder realities of historical instability ("reality TV" exists where there is no privacy).

These paradoxes of time and space in the privately experienced collective event can produce a sense of relief—the domestic site of consumed history seems to slow the pace of the world, along with protecting spectators from scrutiny and the vulnerabilities of encountering people and power outside the home. At the same time, consumer citizenship is always at least one step behind the mass event. The glorious sense of having avoided the risk of being vulnerable in public or to a public can also be experienced as a feeling of powerlessness and irrelevance, for if one can mainly watch and listen, or if one refuses to participate in the "we" that so often accompanies the "feel," one's response has no impact beyond the personal zone. It is a small step from privatized national participation to a sense of political irrelevance to a turning away from politics as a zone of imagined agency, as the vast majority of voting-age Americans have done. Consumer citizenship in this regard draws a line between the degraded political sphere and social membership in the consumer sphere, the realm of pleasures and ordinary survival. The private performance of public emotion in these senses can further isolate subjects from experiencing or challenging the structural and juridical terms of the collectiveness of their collective histories.

If the subject does identify her membership in the public of a larger, often national, public world in terms of her mass-mediated responses to it we can be sure she will be called to experience her affect/opinion in terms of normative moral hierarchies.[9] Where liveness-as-history is concerned, the performative, presentist body genres—sensationalist news and narrative, political melodrama, docutragedy and docucomedy, for example—shuttle between negative emotions related to personally felt threat and scenes that sustain and give moral distinction to attachments to the comforts of normativity even if the conditions for the ideal-normative good life have not actually existed.[10] Any consequences of this shifting relation for a given event are historically specific, of course. But the paradox of the political culture of true feeling—that the experience of historical liveness relies on a sense that private visceral activity is at the core of political participation—is especially active in modern, liberal nationalisms.

By "true feeling" I refer to an argument I've made elsewhere, that around 1830 a shift in emphasis with respect to the ethics of Enlightenment subjectivity emerged in the elite sectors of the United States, which challenged rationality as the core activity distinguishing the human being.[11] Supplanting the universal primacy of human cognition was an image of the person as a subject with moral feeling, and especially with a capacity for feeling and responding to the suffering of less fortunate others who could be described not as individuals but as members of a subordinated population.[12] In contrast to the project of constitutional universalism, which focused on the simultaneity of individual and national autonomy and self-development, the growth of the liberal state in response to antislavery, feminist, and pro–indigenous rights activism (among other forces) was an effect of the promotion of pain capacity as the ground of the human as such.

The universalization of pain made a new pathway to citizenship. Social activists came to demand of free citizens a kind of moral cognition that the perception of injustice means nothing without compassion, and compassion was seen as a public emotion, as a motive for transformative practice. An idea that all subjects were emotionally identical in their pain and suffering and therefore imaginable by each other became the basis of arguments for national belonging; at the same time, the coming-to-precedence of visceral politics required the presumption that certain affective responses came to humans from something like natural law, such that to feel emotion *x* in response to injustice was to be morally authorized in the political sphere.

Behind all this is the Christian religious sense of compassion as a fundamental social ligament. In the Protestant entailment woven through U.S. constitutional and liberal theory, this relational affect was thought to bring one enough into the experience of others such that one comes to understand their destiny as tied in with one's own. Social transformation, in this view, was not at root a structural event but an emotional one: one's availability to experience identification with a capacity for experience located *inside* the subordinated other would lead one to desire uplift or emancipation for that person or population. This sentimental moral psychology became a vehicle for delivering virtue to the privileged, who got to feel good about themselves for having the appropriate feelings about a subordinated kind of person or population. At the same time, unsurprisingly, sentimental solicitation has been an extremely effective motor of social change, challenging and extending operative definitions of the human.

As time has passed, a metadiscourse about true feeling has developed. During the twentieth century a visceral, visual version of the U.S. political sphere tapped into the spectacular aspects of what Tom Gunning has called the "cinema of attractions." Gunning argues that early cinema's grammar of attractions was exhibitionist, articulated around the real as spectacle. The cinematic sign was fundamentally there to be seen and internalized as immediate experience, even if the represented world was far from the one in which the spectator lived, and despite the notions of causality and change so central to what became the narrativity of "classic" Hollywood cinema.[13] In turn, television has elaborated these norms of what we might call emotional humanism, relying on the successful broadcast of scenes of intense emotion to serve as a lubricant for a particular experience of social belonging—whether in the terms of the "traditional" patriotic National Symbolic, the carceral state, a polity of television consumers, or a collection of free autonomous individuals living in a mass-mediated simultaneity.[14] This is why the emotional transparency of melodrama is so central to the docudramatic production and dissemination of a generalized publicness. The airwaves are saturated with incitements to keep citizens linked to each other through the belief that the version of experience they see digested on-screen is composed of their own, the public's own, simultaneous, spontaneous, identical, and fully fleshed-out sensations in response to events deemed clearly worthy of noticing in a particular way.

Melodramatic reality genres, generating a thread of affect that binds consumers to multiple kinds of publicness, emphasize the ethical and political demands of the negative emotions, especially in the domain of pain. The experience of self-disrupting, subjective, and socially rooted pain has become such a universalizing force that any individual's emotions of social discomfort can be argued for as transparent self-evidence for the existence of injustice. Now it is possible for anyone to claim that challenges to their desire for an unconflicted world have produced the kind of pain that ought to set in motion the recuperative justice implied by the moral-affective contract of liberal personhood and politics I've just described. As though all pain were equivalently evidence of injustice, this view authorizes the kind of moral outrage previously deemed appropriate only in response to structural oppression. Elsewhere I have noted the emergence of this "subject of imperiled privilege" during the era of Reaganite cultural politics. This subject, not structurally subordinated, radiates sanctity and sanctimony: the liberal religious genealogy of the culture of true feeling reemerges as moral outrage when the privileged no longer feel secure as worthy of default respect or deference.[15]

Political theorist Wendy Brown has claimed recently that what we might call the moral turn abets left and progressive political paralysis as well as right-wing power consolidation.[16]

> While moralizing discourse symptomizes impotence and aimlessness with regard to making a future, it also marks a peculiar relationship to history, one that holds history responsible, even morally culpable, at the same time as it evinces a disbelief in history as a teleological force. When belief in the continuity and forward movement of historical forces is shaken, even as those forces appear so powerful as to be very nearly determining, the passionate political will is frustrated in all attempts to gain satisfaction at history's threshold: it can acquire neither an account of the present nor any future there. The perverse triple consequence is a kind of moralizing *against* history in the form of condemning particular events or utterances, personifying history in individuals, and disavowing history as a productive or transformative force.

Brown complains here about left moralism, an emotionally trumping rhetoric that overvalues the negative emotions over the total critique or positive program and that ends up overfocusing on eradicating the subjective, rather than structural, effects of injustice.

Brown's excellent analysis locates in the left a will to replace the agonism and contradictions evident in historical struggle with a struggle against contradiction itself, and I think she's right to suggest that a politics of moral hierarchy tends to sublimate history onto a field of ahistorical truths. However, her emphasis on the self-undermining of left political practice indicates implicitly that its moralizing tendencies come from internal theoretical or political wrong turns. I have tried to suggest otherwise here. The moral-affective tendency in U.S. politics belongs to no political field per se and has a longer history whose modern presidential watermark is in pro- and anti-FDR polemic, and requires an analysis of the affective norms of the political sphere as such. In particular, we need to understand the consequences of the claim that emotions provide the best material from which determinations about justice are made.

As other essays in this volume suggest, the state inculcation of antifascist and anticommunist feeling during the 1940s and 1950s looms as a direct predecessor of the current state orchestration of antiterror emotion. During the 1950s many dissenting intellectuals and artists were publicly and tacitly presumed to be un-American, inhuman, perverse, and/or evil—not for refusing the centrality of pain to the definition of the human but for *refusing to agree that a domain of unquestionable moral clarity extended from that pain,* a moral clarity from which a particular project of justice could be advanced. This view did not comprise anti-intellectualism as such, but the only knowledge and aesthetic production deemed worthy was that which supported the anticommunist/Cold War moral view. Now we have moved from "The only thing we have to fear is fear itself"[17] to visions of Terror as the central feeling of our historical moment.[18] For all sorts of reasons, the contemporary shift does not merely repeat the earlier developments in state emotionalism. Still, to understand the Bush administration's vernacular of the viscera, its effort to put forth politics as the practice of moral transparency rather than juridical validity, we need some sense of the genealogy of consensual practices to which we have become accustomed in the U.S. political sphere.

What does it mean to measure the scale of an event or scene through an emotional epistemology? How has the convention of elaborating moral stances from an ostensibly transparent emotional experience shaped the orchestration of crisis in U.S. politics? Anticommunist and antiterror(ist) campaigns related to the fear of foreigners who have surreptitiously breached the national boundaries have marked central moments in the normalizing of state emotionalism as a strategy of social binding in the U.S. political sphere. This essay archives three cases for nuancing these questions. The first uses the 1943 film *Tender Comrade* to look at a state-approved style of visceral politics introduced by the fascist crises of the 1930s and beyond; the second at the example of HUAC as the scene of the right's implementation of outrage for visceral politics; the last at the current administration's media campaign to use terror to terrorize and pacify the polity, and to motivate it to delegate knowledge to the state.

Tender Comrade

In the 1943 film *Tender Comrade,* four women with soldier husbands pool their wages in order to rent a comfortable house in which to wait for their men to return. Although of different ages, classes, and ethnic origins, the women know each other from work in what the film showcases as a spectacularly modernist Douglas Aircraft plant, all light and hygienic and cathedral-like. In contrast, the home that they keep is thoroughly Victorian, a virtual diorama of nostalgic housekeeping. But this disjuncture in historical style goes only style-deep. Both spaces endorse a nationalist project that involves the women's embrace of democracy as discipline, with its techniques of the self oriented to the liberal project of the General Will.

> *Helen (Patricia Collinge):* It's only fair to point out that we're all different people and there might be a clash of personalities occasionally—we'd have to find some way of adjusting any disputes that come up.
> *Jo (Ginger Rogers):* Why, that ought to be simple. We could take a vote! We could run the joint like a democracy! And if anything comes up we could call a meeting. . . . Share and share alike.[19]

During the red-baiting season of the decade after 1947, these lines in *Tender Comrade* were brandished as evidence that a subterranean social movement of seditious artist-communists had infiltrated Hollywood with the purpose of infecting national fantasy. In particular, Leila Rogers testified to the House Un-American Activities Committee that her daughter, Ginger ("Jo Jones"), had demonstrated real patriotism in objecting to the subversive proximity of the word "democracy" to "share and share alike."

Rogers maintained that through this exchange and others *Tender Comrade* intended to lure the American audience to associate the optimism of love plots with the anticipation of socialism, and the practical agency of homemaking with the "practice of equality."[20] No matter that the federal Office of War Information had actually *supervised* the production of *Tender Comrade,* deeming it an excellent example of pro-war propaganda for its depiction of women's wartime proprieties;[21] no matter that the title, *Tender Comrade,* comes not from a communist screed but the anodyne Robert Louis Stevenson poem "My Wife."[22] Dalton Trumbo, the author of these lines, was blacklisted in Hollywood from 1947 through 1960, serving eleven months in prison for contempt of Congress. (He refused to name names.) But the film's message about the relation of the personal and the political is actually far more incoherent than this national capitalist/national socialist narrative would suggest.

Among the many stock female housemate characters is a hard woman and adulteress, Barbara Taylor (Ruth Hussey), who dates men on the domestic front while her Casanova husband is in the navy dallying, she presumes, with a woman in every port. Taylor refuses her patriotic duty to pass the war abstemiously working with women and waiting for her man to return. But amidst the tangle of tough girl language and brazen gesture, small facial shots of flickering upset reveal to the audience that Taylor is a softie, and not too far beneath the surface. The housemates, though, cannot read her subtle signs and hector her constantly for overenjoying sex, lipstick, meat, and other rationed sensual and oral pleasures.

In one scene Taylor explodes at her housemates for their intensely normative moral orations on the topic of marriage and militarism, and as she does this she dissents from the sacrificial project of a familialized U.S. nationalism.

> This thing wouldn't have happened in the first place if we were minding our own business. . . . Even the government doesn't know what it's going to do tomorrow. . . . Blow hot, blow cold, he's up, he's down: What kind of business is that anyway? And while we're being pushed around at home our guys are out fighting in countries they haven't even heard of

> for a lot of foreigners who'll turn on us like a pack of wolves the minute it's over.

Jo Jones (Rogers), the film's equally strident protagonist, responds to her intimate enemy.

> You ought to be ashamed of yourself. Do you know where that kind of talk comes from? It comes straight from Berlin. Every time you say, every time you even think it, you're double-crossing your own husband. . . . How can we go on minding our own business when somebody blackjacks us in an alley, you got Pearl Harbor on your hands? And who wants to get slick and fat when half of the people in the world are starving to death of things that we can do without? Mistakes, sure we make mistakes! Plenty of 'em. You want a country where they won't stand for a mistake? Go to Germany! Go to Japan! And the first time you open your trap like you have tonight you'll find a gun in your stomach! You're the kind of people Hitler counted on when he started this war! Talk, talk, talk, and never think. And that's the biggest mistake any guy ever thought of makin' because there are not enough of you and there are plenty of us.

If we were interested in understanding the film's relation to the historical world in which patriotism and dissent are here debated, we would have a hard time gleaning a coherent worldview from either of the women's speeches. Both speeches are patriotic. While Barbara Taylor is clearly anti-FDR, she performs rhetorically her view of his failure to be politically consistent by mixing up her own different dissenting positions, shuttling between isolationist and xenophobic vagueness, along with voicing the indignation of the little guy who resents being pushed around by the big state. Constructed of a rickety pile of clichés, her oppositional vernacular sounds more like an unfiltered blurt than a considered opinion.

Jo Jones responds in pro-FDR fashion of a sort, lumping together Hitler, Berlin, Japan, and indeed any expressed resistance to the ambitions of U.S. hegemony. In the jumble of phrases Rogers proclaims fascist genocide, military violence, ordinary crimes against property, political dissent, and adultery indistinguishable from each other, fellow travelers tainted by association. Dissenters are dangerous because they do not think, and also because they do think—immorally. Anyway, if you dissent you aid the enemy and subvert your own husband, so it is virtually adulterous and treasonous if you dissent; but if you do, it is a tribute to the United States that you are free to transgress and disagree without getting mugged by the state. And anyway, America will win the war because there are more good guys than bad, and anyway . . .

Predictably, in the film the women's argument gets cut short by the radio, which announces dramatically the death in combat of Taylor's wayward husband. The pro-war patriotic stance wins by a KO. But in the prior moment of polemical vitriol, when all potential impediments to the U.S. project meld into a megaenemy, when the adulterer figures as a marital and a political cheat who performs the threatening collapse of social order during a time of crisis, all transgressions seem reasonably characterized as at the same scale and in the same species of treason. All opposition leads to death; any death suggests the potential end of something else, including the whole system. Such a clustering of distinct things into a relation that makes them appear foundationally interconnected constitutes what Ernesto Laclau and Chantal Mouffe would call "a logic of equivalence."[23] In *Tender Comrade* irrationally articulated patriotic views take on the *sound* of explaining the world equivalently well, but they remain untested because resolved by the brutal *interruptus* of death. Then why bother taking time to depict the women's debate at all, since it turns out to be an episode irrelevant to the succeeding events?

The title *Tender Comrade* telegraphs a relation of private life to political continuity in a way that suggests a heartbeat of tenderness beneath the soldier's tough veneer. But in the United States after 1917 this vernacular sense of *comrade* was inflected toward the sense of the word under Russian communism and international socialism, where *comrade* seemed equivalent with *citizen*, while suggesting economic solidarity as the collective glue rather than individuality or private property. (In 1943 Russia was still a U.S. ally; by 1947 the word *comrade* presumed more ominous tones.) During World War II the film title's metaphor clearly meant to bind women to U.S. patriotism, marking the disposition of daily lives at work and at home as military activity akin to that of the life-and-death struggles of their soldier husbands.

At the same time, though, it turns out that the women citizens the film portrays are ideally wholly private, not quite citizens. If their economic camaraderie does signal a socialist desire on Trumbo's part, the use of the word *comrade* in the film also suggests the informal ways women participate in national culture through the power of intimate bonds. Still, there is a difference between women's bonds with other women and with husbands. The truly *tender* comrade is the husband's best friend, the wife.[24] During the war, women are each other's tender *comrades,* producing material support while waiting for the real thing to come home. In order for the democratic nation to remain strong and free, then, a tender comrade must remain tender, must remain what a woman should be. She can work like a man, and use women in the meanwhile to remain affectively alive. Most important, though, is not what she thinks politically or even what she does but that she maintains *the proper emotional orientation* to the husband and to the nation. For the tender comrade is in a structural position to draw a red thread through the nation from the heart to the head of state. When the adulterous one initiates the collapse of venerated hierarchies of value and order, she violates the social function of marital love ideology, which is to make people experience a legal obligation as an expression of the heart's true desire. To love love is to love the law. In times of political crisis there is no greater love.

In these ways, *Tender Comrade* narrates both marital love and patriotism as in a kind of danger that must be counteracted *emotionally.* In this regard it is a classically liberal text, with its tests of individual good intention.[25] It is also a classically modernist text, for a number of reasons. First, as many scholars and theorists have argued, U.S. modernity has been especially associated with the figure of the woman, insofar as "her story" figures as a material and symbolic problem of distinctly modern appetites and their regulation.[26] Second, the film's relation to narrative is fundamentally psychological, constantly looking for the real "underneath" the woman's surface. This is to say that a certain stress is revealed in the system. The aspect of governmentality most salient during and after the war involved the conscription of citizens not to have secrets, to be transparent to their immediate and national publics.[27] (As Michael Rogin and others point out, the communist could not be racialized effectively, except occasionally as the Asian or the Jew: thus a mass paranoia at the specter of the perversely visibly normal was encouraged.)[28] Yet while the film promotes a scheme of self-policing and social scrutiny, it is also comically and seriously aware that subjects are never transparent to themselves or to each other. It suggests that *because* of the unconscious and the ideological,

Americans were required to monitor even more intensely. The impossibility of transparency makes these models of citizen psychology incommensurate. Sexuality, with its jumble of intentional and irrational practices, comes to figure the dangers to the state of this incommensurateness.

Relevant here is Foucault's claim that a particularly sexualized mode of modern symbolization has used intimate relations to make economic, institutional, aesthetic, and everyday practices appear as fundamentally psychological, emotional, and moral emanations.[29] But even if there is a certain broad historical simultaneity to the emergence of the normal in the domain of the human, these categories are not identical matrices of explanation. This discussion of *Tender Comrade* aims to detail some of the particular political utility of their amalgamation under the rubric of sexuality, seen as that most human thing that disrupts the human. Insofar as sexuality denotes the most intimate of social exchanges, it serves as a vehicle for regulating social interdependency and containing irrationality into a process of individuation. During crisis times, the hegemonic bloc (in this case, the liberal nation) needs citizens to activate patriotic attachment as though it were a psychological mode. At stake in the prosecution within and about *Tender Comrade,* then, is a national-capitalist depiction of power and justice in terms of moral clarities and emotional comforts, one whose shape changes throughout the 1940s and 1950s but whose dedication to national hegemony does not. Justice is depicted as a visceral reaction of individuals, and public debate takes the form of a disagreement about whose transparent feelings best measure the evident state of things. The idea that feelings are transparent to subjects becomes ideologically continuous with the moral claim for the clarities of a certain brand of patriotism.

Thus we might say that the rhetorical incoherence of the women's speeches supports a patriotic cause *not despite but because* they are constructed of cliché clusters. In times of real or manufactured political crisis, it is especially likely that the dead speech of the cliché will return in its ghostly garb not only as senseless farce, but also as a genuine and interested attempt to create continuity with the precrisis world. In this way some potentially destabilizing aspects of the crisis being managed can be neutralized or even reclothed as stabilities. Meanwhile, marital love, national patriotism, private property, and freedom to dissent can appear to be linked structurally because as *ideological* clichés—ways of life that carry normative weight—and in ordinary syntax, they are placed in rhetorical proximity to each other. In this way German and Japanese aggression can become phrased as an adulterous instance of personal violation, a gun in the national stomach, a mugging on a global scale. The clarity of the cliché cluster converted to moral metaphor claims to express a deeper and higher truth than the surfaces of rationality can provide. The cliché is to moral political rhetoric what the true feeling is to emotional humanism: together they produce an image of citizen subjectivity oriented around a defensive attachment to convention.

This is why anyone who says otherwise, who asks for "nuance" or seeks to measure degrees of magnitude, is to be revealed as a dangerous thinker. Mass politics of the twentieth century has witnessed the formation of a mode of political performativity that conventionalizes particular tones of voice as themselves guarantors of the truths that a "we" know emotionally even if our clarities are tangled up with false intellectual claims by those who dare to brandish nuance in the face of what a moral person deeply already knows. A thinker is deemed threatening when a particular historical bloc needs its view of order both to be taken for granted and to be newly embraced, in a kind of recommitment ritual. When nationalists use marital compliance not only as an analogy for but also a mechanism of patriotic solidarity, they seek to establish their view as not merely just and morally right but also as an ahistorical value that needs to be reanimated in practice. The moral obligations of love do not require the "nuance" of rational argument; in fact, such nuance is a transgression against the higher truth that anyone interested in truth could see and should desire. In contrast, the dissenting thinker seems deliberately to refuse to acknowledge the moral and emotional clarities a good person would seek. Dangerous thinkers, in this view, might as well be destroying love as challenging the state.

I have suggested that, in *Tender Comrade,* the moral adjudication of virtue and subversion is vocalized in political incoherence on all sides. The nonevent status of the women's debate illustrates its conventionality, but more than that too. Trumbo decries the early-twentieth-century right-wing "degrading process of politics-as-magic and incantation-as-intellect"; in the modern United States, debate is equally and paradoxically monologic. The political sphere is manifested through the serial performance of one passionate rant after another, at the scale of authoritarian passion with divaesque sentimental or melodramatic tonalities. Indeed, in the contemporary scene the word *rant,* popularized by the comedian Dennis Miller, has become the predominant genre for the public expression of political opinion. Many other political films manifest the same convention: partly parodically, no doubt (to the extent that mainstream politics is deemed to generate meaningless or prevaricating speech), but also, I contend, because at stake is not the idea being promoted but the emotional threat and payoff performed. Thus while we may not be surprised by the incoherence of political rhetoric, it would be a mistake to think of these rhetorical messes as failures to produce articulate persuasion. The pitting of a moral epistemology against a rational one via a notion of authentic emotion is a rhetorical political convention for the production of what Gramsci calls "passive revolution." Passive revolution is a vehicle for producing mass consent to a view as though it were already taken for granted and should need no arguing for.[30] Ethicoemotional performance in the political sphere clearly aims to instantiate such a guarantee.

Elaine Hadley has suggested that a "melodramatic mode" of political speech saturated Late Victorian England, before the electronic media recorded the grain of the voice but at the same time that the political sphere absorbed a much larger and more class-diverse polity.[31] She argues that melodramatic conventions of political theatricality were crucial to the political sphere for a number of reasons, two of which seem relevant to this essay's more modern genealogical attempt. Hadley argues that melodrama was the favorite mode of popular theater in nineteenth-century England, a popularity that stood in direct contrast with the equally emotional but more elite containments of romantic poetry. Thus if the eighteenth century saw political satire as its chosen hyperbolic genre of critique, during the nineteenth century expanding political participation relied on a more popular genre to mark out the field of power.

Hadley also points out that during this period the British state was beginning to taxonomize and rank its populations more meticulously and discriminatingly than it had done in preindustrial times. The enumeration of populations through census and other modes of categorization can be read as the dialectical other of the hyperemotional political rhetoric she describes as "the melodramatic mode." As we will see, this dialectic is visible again during the Cold War and at the present moment. The iconicity of a designated enemy is constituted by its supposed veiledness, its open secrecy—whether behind the Iron Curtain, in caves and cells, or through networks of spies and mobile phones. Thus when historians of the Cold War talk about the ideology of "containment," we can read the metaphor strongly, as a state will-to-formalism that also intensified a ravenous paranoia whose epistemological hunger must never be satisfied.[32] This is why, as Ellen Schrecker and others have archived stunningly, universities and the entertainment industry were deemed sites of a potentially spreading counterhegemonic negativity. It was feared that an antidemocratic, anti-American ideology was being made desirable through the pleasures of entertainment and the authority of academic knowledge. In response to this fear of left-wing magic, the state-located affect culture of the United States that disseminated this view took on a bizarre, counterintuitive shape. Dating from the rise of the House Un-American Activities Committee, rhetorical norms of melodramatic political affect contravened the message of state rationality or coolness. The "terror" produced by secret insurgents reappeared as a virtually homeopathic threat in the grandstanding of members of the hegemonic bloc, whose actuarial fictionalizing and polemical grandiosity is realistically reproduced in *The Manchurian Candidate.* Images of Senator Joseph McCarthy waving pieces of paper, yelling "point of order" in a disorderly manner, condense this paradoxical political style. The televised hearings show the range of McCarthy's moral outrage, from passionately emotional tones to understated threatening ones: witnesses arguing for shame and decency in response were actually confirming that this war for the national (political) heart was an emotional one. Each side's tonality seeks performatively to enact its claim of emotional authenticity, telegraphing a personal connection to a suprapolitical truth on which U.S. democracy is said to depend.

The House Un-American Activities Committee

The historian Eli Zaretsky locates the origin of right-wing polemical sentimentality in the three anticommunist hysterias of the early century, dating from around 1917, 1930, and then throughout the 1950s, the period in which HUAC did its most effective work.[33] Zaretsky argues that the right's desire to defeat the New Deal has since organized a mode of hysterical antipolitical politics. Red-baiting stirs up an image of the fearless courageous patriot who looks strong by refusing the status quo of soft appearances and tough deceptions. As the shapeless enemy infiltrates the ranks of power, slowly and secretly shifting its norms toward treason and perversion of the American Way of Life, the radical conservative embraces outrage in all its tonalities to protect the passivity of the innocent American, otherwise seduced or taken unawares.

Appropriately for historians of the present as a liveness-effect, the HUAC hearings were the first political trials of the twentieth century televised live to a mass audience. In this early moment of you-are-there visual national experience, in which the state's embodiment in official persons became evident to millions of citizens simultaneously, what appeared was not what Peter Stearns has called American Cool, with its bourgeois sense of measure and scale, but a political style of aggressive conservative affect on behalf of a sentimental national character so fragile it needed guarding by ferocious martinets.[34] While the cause of law and order provided the explicit referent, political style took on a humanist-populist guise of visceral emotionality, associating conservativism and proper patriotism with belief in and access to the higher common sense of the deeper human truths.

In contrast to the vernacular incoherence of the women arguing politics in *Tender Comrade,* the political vernacular of political elites during the Cold War married moral panic and rationality. An excellent specimen of this idiom of power is available in this HUAC document, the opening sentences of which chronicle a meeting of artists and intellectuals in New York City in 1954.

> Parading under the imposing title of the Scientific and Cultural Conference for World Peace the gathering at the Waldorf-Astoria Hotel in New York City on March 25, 26, and 27th 1949, was actually a supermobilization of the inveterate wheelhorses and supporters of the Communist Party and its auxiliary organizations. It was in a sense a glorified pyramid club, pyramiding into one inflated front the names which had time and again been used by the Communists as decoys for the entrapment of innocents. The Communist-front connections of these sponsors, as reflected by the tabulation in this report, are very extensive. One person has been affiliated with at least 85 Communist-front organizations. Three persons have been affiliated with from 71 to 80 Communist-front organi-

> zations; 4 have been affiliated with from 51–60 communist-front organizations; 8 have been affiliated with from 41–50; 10 have been affiliated with from 31–40; 28 have been affiliate with from 21–30, and 234 have been affiliated with from 1–10 Communist-front organizations.

This document, the *Review of the Scientific and Cultural Conference for World Peace,* stunningly locates long lists of numbers and names along with paranoia about secrecy, front organizations, decoys, and other modes of false entrapment technology. Celebrities and intellectuals on the left are defined as soldier aggressors in a culture war who fight dirty by deploying the higher and lower pleasures—excess measured as the *n*-th degree of resistance. In this mode the excessive fact list is the moral truth in contrast to artists' immoral critical reflections: HUAC locates the scale of the event by swinging between foregrounding a potential miasma of antinormative, antinational excess and the stack of hot numerical facts. I have suggested that McCarthy, like many anticommunist rhetoricians, was a master of emotional performance: mobilizing disgust and outraged moral clarity, he marked paranoia as the appropriate response of the just mind to the deviousness of the unjust and manifested the triumph of facts in the face of the explicit and hidden deceits of the dissenters. The FBI's documents deploy this emotional epistemology as well and likewise bolster the affect with a kind of taxonomic and enumerative frenzy.

What's crucial to understand here is that hyperbolic state emotionalism and pseudopositivism are cast as exaggerated to the degree to which the secret, invisible dissenters have pushed the state. This is why has been useful for me to think about the emotionality of our contemporary nation-state relation in terms of the prior anticommunist moment. Then, as now, an incoherent and skewed jumble of oppositions between patriotic sentiment and dissenting dogmatism, patriotic resolve and dissenting weakness, and the openness of democracy and the secrecy of terror/communism were mobilized by power elites in the political public sphere. Then, as now, the emotional clarities of the powerful sought to shame out of existence the kinds of open argument and dissent that make nations live democracies in practice. As now, the suspension of the spirit and letter of democratic law was deemed not to be a proactive program of constraining liberty but an emergency suspension of law in order to save the law from secret subversion.

Infinite Justice, the War on Terror, and the Fear of Formlessness

Recent work on HUAC describes anticommunism as a concern that played a relatively small role in the lives of subjects and citizens who had no access to the kinds of economic and institutional power and influence of political elites and insiders.[35] In contrast, public responses to the attack on the WTC and the Pentagon distinguish themselves through a style of moral psychology more explicitly centered in notions of faith- and community-based norms. In the public rhetoric that emerged during and after the events, the mix of emotionality and positivism of the Cold Warriors persisted, but this time the orchestration came from the televisual and radio journalists before the state had a chance to pull itself together. One result of this shock of actually live liveness is that the emotional tone of the collective response was set normatively prior to any responses in terms of policy. Greg Myers's work on the production of the American vox populi shows that it was as though the putative transparency and hardwiredness of emotion was the event, or at least the event the audience could understand, about which we could first know facts: immediately the press used the language of "we," of "our feelings" and of an "our history" that presumed the global viewing public to have become "American" post-traumatically (as *Le Monde* went on to say) by virtue of having witnessed the violent anti-American trespassing on U.S. territory.[36] Please note that I am describing the centrality of emotional experience to the production of patriotic publicness, not saying that there was something scandalous in the immediate normativity of affective nation-(re)building that went on in and was recorded by the media. Not scandalous at all, in fact: it was the business of feeling national as usual.

Quickly, though, the administration borrowed the sensationalist energy from the media's nationalization of trauma. The subjects of imperiled privilege were this time identified *tout court* as ordinary innocent "Americans," and the Bush administration repeatedly equated justice with the demolition of the (at first) unnamed and invisible perpetrators who created Americans as a species haunted by the Terror. Meanwhile, his administration assumed the rights to all satellite photographs from Afghanistan, asked the press not to show live pictures of any of the terrorists, and kept secret and without due process the prisoners they took during the wars from Afghanistan and the

United States—and while developing the terror muscle of the body politic, the administration underfunded the office of Homeland Security and any project of national defense put forth in its name.

Deleuze and Guattari argue that paranoia is the appropriate subjective response to the iconic hypervisibility of the fascist state; from the contemporary U.S. governmental perspective, paranoiac moralizing is the appropriate response to the opposite condition, dissenting invisibility.[37] Terrorized, the state performs a feeling of sudden national boundary collapse from fear that the enemy is not one but many, not somewhere but everywhere, not located but mobile, not identifiable but protean, not just isolated but woven into the fabric of everyday life. The war is on terror and not simply fear because fear has an object, while terror leaks potentially into all spaces of experience. The administration then asked citizens to feel terrorized too, and likewise to be hypervigilant in everyday life, taking up position as the state's disciplinary deputies. In other words, whether or not it makes sense to call fascistic the government's defiance of the letter and spirit of U.S. civil rights and international law during this period, it claims to be mimetic. Its embrace of secrecy as security is mimetic as well. As the Enemy is perceived to have no shape, to produce an enigmatic and therefore lawless anti-American crusade, then the U.S. state too must assume a kind of hyperbolic formlessness. The War on Terror renders that aura of dissolution and promises, at the same time, to return transparency—form, boundary, law, and the normative way of life—to the world once the shapeless dark forces have been defeated.

Predictably, as the two towers fell and melted on 9/11/01, an actuarial imaginary uncannily similar to that of the HUAC mentality took shape in the U.S. public sphere: so many killers, so many dead, so much property value wasted, so many tons of garbage, so much more of x and so much less of y, where x = U.S. righteousness, patriotism, insecurity, anger, and trauma and y = U.S. innocence, ignorance, naïveté, security, civil liberties, freedoms, and so on. The numbers kept changing, but the comfort of actuarial proclamations seemed to assure knowledge and the continuity of U.S. imperial agency amidst the improvisation that trauma inevitably causes. Daily the State Department issued a color code (Code Red, Code Yellow, etc.) that tells us how intense our terror of terror should be on any given day. The broadcast of these codes was not accompanied by strategies for surviving actual violence. Be terrified of what you don't know, but leave the knowing to the state; meanwhile, the state acts rationally when it can but assumes the moral and political right to trump counterarguments with emotional clarities and law with enigmatic policies in order to defeat the morally public but bureaucratically secret and terrifyingly spreading anti-American forces.

This dialectic between what's frighteningly formless and the statistical production of quasi-already normative reality saturates the nongovernmental posttraumatic scene in the United States as well. For instance, following on discussions about reparation to unjustly treated Native, Japanese, and African Americans, a public conflict persists about whether the families of those killed in New York and Washington deserve payment, about how many millions each life lost is worth, and to which person the worth goes. A similar question of corporate rather than corporeal reparation was raised with respect to the airline and insurance industries, as well as for New York City itself. When ordinary people are killed as innocent Americans, tort law and a utopian tradition of cultural guilt for national wrongs converge in a flood of uncertainty as to the ethics of actuarial judgment.

In stark relief to this frenzy of value assignation, the negative space where the buildings were is termed Ground Zero, and in stark contrast again the U.S. military response was, at first, called Infinite Justice. News conferences are held where predictions as to the cost of the war are pronounced, then revised. Then there is the nationalist drama of the interest rate, the stock market, the recession and recovery, with their jerky dynamics and magical qualities that seem to denote futures or even faith in national and global boom and bust. And then there are the presidential approval poll figures. That numbers keep changing matters not: we may be balancing on a bubble, but whether it bursts, leaks slowly, or continues to expand, what will matter is that this mathematical antisublime keeps shaping the terms of the quid pro quo in the political public sphere in the spirit of a posttraumatic lex talionis, an eye for an eye, a primitive contract shaping the rhetorical terms of just revenge by reference to traumatic woundings of the flesh. In short, enumeration is central to constituting the national present as a continuous site of urgency, in which experts encourage hunting, gathering, and hoarding value against Terror's shapeless negative effectivity.

Mary Poovey writes that this tendency to name, number, and make accounts as modes of accounting for vast social phenomena is intricately involved with what counts as modernity.[38] Normativity, the statistical ballast for capitalist flux offered up by the census and the tax roll made it possible to draw a line at a particular time/space called the *here and now;* in this space modern identity would appear as a standardized ratio of intelligible qualities and the modern state as a set of property relations and reciprocal obligations. Normativity describes the ways that these facts of social being came to seem like social being's foundation, the basis of personal and collective continuity. Modernist normativity was about, as they say, time passing into an unprecedented sensorium, aesthetic or Fordist, autonomous or exploited, those dialectical pairs whose continuities in the optimism of ideologies of mobility or self-cultivation made the past into something that happened long ago.

In contrast, postmodern geographers suggest that the post-Fordist world of the present, also disorganized by capitalist flux, operates according to an unprecedented degree of time/space compression and an incitement to speed up, a phenomenon akin to liveness.[39] In this regime of experience the present is not a contained or unprecedented space of time but one that calls out religious and science fiction metaphors about living in continuous alternative chronologies that tend all too intensely toward the contingent and the sublime. Pasts leak into futures and vice versa in a way that threatens to destroy the capacity to live historically, in a material way, leading to intensified problems of survival. I detail three kinds here.

First, a powerful sense that power is deracinated, organized elsewhere in some nonreciprocal offshore location or in the cave of a shadow government, rubs up against a sense that lived spaces continue to matter more than the power that has no face. This means either that the value of the local is constantly felt to be expropriated by national capitalist/global formations or that the local is felt to survive in the authentic habits and habitations of ordinary people despite the expropriation of their labor value by capital, "Empire," or that old saw, the ruling classes. Any point on the local/global grid so imagined is, at the same time, a point of political powerlessness and irrelevance. That the Bush Jr. administration deifies the local in contrast to the national participates in the affective rhetoric of apolitical and ahistorical moral clarity that the right wing wants to attach to national patriotism.

The second survival blockage concerns the identity form, or the relation of ethnic, racial, and sexual specificity to singular individuality, often called sovereignty, and often linked with U.S. national identity. At present, and in both directions, this relation of identity (collective subaltern individuality) to singularity (one's specific history, protected as individuality by the national rights form) tends to be marked as a relation of authenticity to depersonalization and violence. Chela Sandoval's *Methodology of the Oppressed* most clearly describes this crisis in the obstacles to a critical experience of the present. She argues that what feels like the current threat to a sense of control by the elite feels like the ordinary conditions of consciousness and survival among the subordinated classes.[40] The events of September 11 further intensified the anger of the privileged at being made to feel constrained in their treatment of historical minorities: if we are all, more than ever, Americans, why do the subalterns and liberals insist on creating fissures that need not be there?[41] As a result the structural inequality that governs everyday life in the United States is drowned out in battles over symbolization, and identity politics is misidentified as an elite movement in contrast to the vernacularity of Anglo-American supremacy.

Third, this crisis in historicity and social connectedness works well for the maintenance and reproduction of the hegemonic bloc, for the regime where a sense of local cultural and economic ordinariness that feels manageable, resistant to capitalist appropriation, and irrelevant to the political mainstream works beautifully to enable the increasing consolidation of wealth in the hands of a very few global citizens and corporations. At the same time, this sense of comfortable, contained, and controllable ordinariness can be remobilized at any time as newly vulnerable to a crisis in the present that demands a new citizen sensorium on behalf of the collective or national continuity that protects what has been designated the taken-for-granted, the social conditions for the experience of that mirage of normativity's naturalness. In short, the taken-for-granted or normative labor of the ordinariness that is ordinal is said now to be so at risk that a state of emergency must exist for the foreseeable present, which is synonymous, in times of crisis, with the foreseeable future. (In this regard, the world in which public numbers are deemed neutral is at risk in the same sense that clichés seem at risk: the desire to return to the world before crisis is displayed as a desire for dead facts or transparent truths.)

How is the idiom of affective nationality related to a contemporary politics of ordinariness, then, and what is its relation to the liveness of mass trauma and the vernacularization of politics? Usually ordinary locality is manifest in the sense that events are continuous, taking place in a flow of, to use Bourdieu's phrase, "practical activity oriented toward practical functions."[42] I am arguing that the mass experience of national vulnerability reveals what was already true, that both workers and ordinary property owners were never in control of the conditions of their continuity and value. But because this time the logic of that contingency is not capitalist, but national, the ordinary is redefined as that horizon of the taken-for-granted that is protected by national sovereignty. The Bush administration wants the nation form deemed central to the survival of ordinary life, while hiding its commitment to the reproduction of structural (economic) inequality. Thus follows the right-wing argument that the nation can go on securing the right to feel autonomous, local, self-sovereign, and ultimately unhampered by the political only if the administration proceeds unopposed.

Tom Dumm argues that ordinariness usually coordinates multiple temporalities that flow into each other as the taken-for-granted, but which nonetheless are not entirely continuous, but contrapuntal and shadowy. Memory, habit, labor, practice, fantasy, all the processes involved in the reproduction of life—the chaos that might ensue from this jumble of temporalities is shaped by the ways normative modes of subjective tracking locate continuity in particular cross-sections of stories that impact personal and public versions of the self, sometimes to fray their distinctions and other times to insist on them. In contrast, national trauma is ordinariness's other in that it is a scene of the experience of enmeshed distinctions too. At stake in the posttraumatic citizenship ideology of the moment is a project of making citizens who actively feel, and feel political, but only on behalf of their future reprivatization. National sentimentality frequently works against the political in exactly this way.

The genre of liveness most symptomatic of the depoliticization of patriotic politics is most available on the cable news networks. Regardless of whatever particular diegetic news is being broadcast on any given televisual news outlet, we can now expect that the stock ticker, long a convention of the representation of capitalist instability in the public sphere, will reappear as a news ticker, a conveyance for sentences about simultaneous events that may, on reflection, seem of all different scales but which have been flattened out as urgent messages streaming below the image. Colin Powell in Palestine is propped next to a baseball score, and succeeding that is news of the opening of the internet kiosk at the Iowa state fair, a dog show in New Mexico, new news about diet.

Newly nationalized biography became similarly factualized, as for six months after September 11 the *New York Times* published a daily segment called *The Nation Stunned,* containing a series of pictures, each decked with a biographical caption, describing the ways a given deceased occupant of the World Trade Center was good, loved and loveable, and had ordinary habits and dreams, and who therefore deserved, after all, to have lived. There is no reason to do a close reading of these stories or the images that they accompany. The scale of this personhood genre made it possible for any reader to identify with these people, who represent not abjection or *bare life* at all, but potential human value unrealized.

All of the occupants of that building complex have not yet been so narrated, and the obituarial series has now been made into an occasional piece. The cessation of the imperative to witness daily the value of these lost lives suggests that, from the *New York Times*'s point of view, at least, it became time for the public to pass into something almost beyond the event—posttraumatic, but not quite ordinary in the old sense. Actually, starting from three days after the event, newspapers and newsreaders conveyed the president's view that it was time to return to business as usual, although business would never be usual again. Why did the nation/state/media want people to slouch toward ordinariness? First and foremost, citizens were said to have a duty as consumers to bolster the economy that both performs U.S. health and consolidates U.S. wealth in a way that stabilizes its sovereignty among nations. This decaying margin, this calendar of convoluted histories, this timeline of territorialized events, was sutured to ordinariness almost instantly by both the televisual intensity of September 11 and the insistence that consumers, after all, needed to vote for American freedom by intense amounts of shopping. New markets in flag paraphernalia burst out everywhere. But most important to the success of the state project was that as the subject reemerged into ordinariness she or he felt viscerally transformed toward the practice of proper citizenship. Protest was seen as treasonous; but appearing on the street as a typical citizen of capital, a producer and consumer, was given the highest regard.

To summarize, at present the political sphere of the United States is saturated by the deployment of emotion to convert the nation from the liveness of politics to the time of moral clarities that actively trump nuancing dissenting counternarratives. Along with consolidating national power, this emotional epistemology creates a decaying border where sovereign subjects are hailed to experience an astigmatism in the patriotic gaze, a posttraumatic, terrorized perspective from which one looks back on a time of moral innocence, acts free in small, ordinary ways, and continues to feel historically saturated by an immediacy now less and less grounded in unusual practices of monitoring on CNN or Fox military violence or the cleanup at Ground Zero. From this fold in time one remembers the initial impact in a visceral way but feels overwhelmed by considerations of ongoing practical agency in response to the stimulus of injustice. Those matters have been appropriated by the right-wing government, whose aim is to represent the public in a moral-emotional way, bracketing representation of the more socially conflictual debates about who deserves what resources.

Harnessing public feeling to the moral clarities of the parallel universe where faith and evil battle it out can generate a certain consoling rhythm that makes it possible to count the everyday as the space of survival, shedding a real-time social imagination of a better good life. But the end of the count, 3–2–1, signals not the end of the bad time but the beginning of bad time, the polity reeling (or should I say *realing*) from so many technical knockouts as the state abrogates laws, rights, and norms of justice on behalf of its fight against the very Terror it foments, live. In this administration, the state markets such emotion as the space where authentic voting takes place. Consumers of history's live parade, living in the astigmatic, mismatched, jagged domains of the new forced ordinariness, holding on to the domestic ballast of the everyday, we are asked to participate in the mass intimacy of strangers across a political sphere in which the political is delegated to leaders who lead us away from the instabilities of nuance while feeling as comfortable as sheep who are counted on the way to political sleep.

NOTES

Thanks very much to Jackie Stacey, Mark Miller, Austin Sarat, my Lancaster grad seminar, and the anonymous readers for help with this thing.

1. Jacques Rancière, *On the Shores of Politics (Phronesis),* trans. Liz Heron (New York: Verso, 1995), 11.

2. Peggy Noonan, "A Chat in the Oval Office," *Wall Street Journal Online,* June 25, 2001; ITV, April 4, 2002, republished online by the U.S. Department of State's Office of International Information Programs at usinfo.state.gov.

3. See, for example, "I think things can be over-nuanced," Press Secretary Ari Fleischer, April 29, 2002; National Security Advisor Condoleezza Rice: "We can never let the intricacies of cloistered debate—with its many hues of gray and nuance—obscure the need to speak and act with moral clarity" (April 29, 2002; http://www.whitehouse.gov/news/releases/2002/04/20020429-9.html). On the other side, tens of thousands of anti-Bush Google hits register the ironies of "nuance": for example, Jim Lobe, "Alternative realities in the Bush White House," *Asia Times,* April 23, 2002, at http://www.atimes.com/front/DD23Aa02.html; Jon Young, *Waco Times,* September 28, 2001, "Upon reflection, choosing warring words a little more carefully."

4. See Jürgen Habermas, *The Structural Transformation of the Public Sphere* (Cambridge: MIT Press, 1991), for an argument about the classic form of publicness and its decline in the twentieth century as participation in the political sphere shifted from the deprivatization of opinion to a more passive spectatorship. See also Douglas Kellner, "Habermas, the Public Sphere, and Democracy: A Critical Intervention," at http://www.gseis.ucla.edu/faculty/kellner/kellner.html.

5. This conceptualization of the nation as an affective public, and currently a sphere of intimacy, derives largely from my national sentimentality project, available most visibly in *The Anatomy of National Fantasy* (Chicago: University of Chicago Press, 1991) and *The Queen of America Goes to Washington City* (Durham: Duke University Press, 1997). Additionally, there is now a national consortium of "public feelings" cells made up of scholars, artists, and activists, linked by the Feminist Futures project of the University of Chicago, Barnard College, University of Arizona at Tucson, and the University of Texas at Austin's Women's/Gender Studies/Sexuality Centers. For more on the public feelings project, see feeltankchicago.net.

6. I learned this way of phrasing the problem of embodied thought from Elaine Hadley. See Hadley, *Living Liberalism: Signature, Citizens, and Celebrity in Victorian England* (forthcoming). See also David Lloyd and Paul Taylor, *Culture and the State* (New York: Routledge, 1998).

7. On the history of sensation, media, "liveness," and publicness, see Karen Halttunen, *Murder Most Foul: The Killer and the American Gothic Imagination* (Cambridge: Harvard University Press, 2000); Jane Feuer, "The Concept of Live Television: Ontology as Ideology," in *Regarding Television: Critical*

Approaches—An Anthology, ed. E. Ann Kaplan (Los Angeles: American Film Institute, 1983); Mary Ann Doane, "Information, Crisis, Catastrophe," in *Logics of Television: Essays in Cultural Criticism,* ed. Patricia Mellencamp (Bloomington: Indiana University Press, 1990), 222–39; Philip Auslander, *Liveness: Performance in a Mediatized Culture* (New York: Routledge, 1999).

8. The phrase *zone of privacy* is an effect and a symptom of modern political emotionality, with its presumptions that the law ought to follow juridical viscera, deemed representative of human emotion generally. For an analysis of reproductive privacy as a feature of the emotional normativity of modern sexuality, see Lauren Berlant, "The Subject of True Feeling: Pain, Privacy, Politics," in *Cultural Pluralism, Identity Politics, and the Law,* ed. Austin Sarat (Ann Arbor: University of Michigan Press, 2001), 49–84.

9. My primary referent for this account of modernity's impact on the senses is Georg Simmel, "Modernity and Modern Life": in contemporary critical theory, see Miriam Bratu Hansen, "The Mass Production of the Senses," in *Rethinking Film History,* ed. Christine Gledhill and Linda Williams (London: Edward Arnold, 2000), 322–50; and Isobel Armstrong, *The Radical Aesthetic* (London: Blackwell, 2001).

10. All genres are body genres, in the sense that generic conventions promise consumers a return to predictable emotions emplotted in, at least, clever but not too surprising ways.

11. Eric Slauter argues that this shift between rational and emotional rhetoric in the U.S. political sphere takes place during the late eighteenth century, when animal rights activist arguments concerning the ethics of human/nonhuman domination were redeployed to make antislavery arguments. I suggest that this emotional appeal found dominance first in or around 1824, the widely celebrated twenty-fifth anniversary of the U.S. republic's founding, when the nation became officially a referent with a history, and nationalist rhetoric was congealed via parades, spectacles, oratory, and other confirmatory expressions of collective public emotion. Additionally, the nationalization of emotion was advocated powerfully by William Lloyd Garrison's Abolitionist newspaper, *The Liberator* (1833), which saw the commingling of economic, religious, and political arguments with sentimental appeals to middle-class readers, especially women, not to be hard-hearted and to recognize the fundamental affective humanity in the slave's suffering body and soul. The project here was to make visceral the injustice that Native American and African slave occupants of the United States were exiled from the national promise of emancipation, a condition that the Constitution argued ought to be experienced subjectively by all (who counted as) men. See Eric Slauter, "Slavish Imitation: The Circulation of Rights in the Age of the American Revolution" (forthcoming) and "Being Unreasonable in the Age of Reason: The Rights of Animals," Society of Early Americanists, Providence, RI, April 2003.

12. See Berlant, "The Subject of True Feeling."

13. Tom Gunning, *D. W. Griffith and the Origins of American Narrative Film: The Early Years at Biograph* (Urbana: University of Illinois Press, 1994), 41.

14. On the national symbolic as a machine for the management of the nation's ghosted history, see Lauren Berlant, *The Anatomy of National Fantasy* (Chicago: University of Chicago Press, 1991).

15. On "imperiled privilege," see Lauren Berlant, *The Queen of America Goes to Washington City: Essays on Sex and Citizenship* (Durham: Duke University Press, 1997).

16. Wendy Brown, "Moralism as Antipolitics," in *Materializing Democracy: Toward a Revitalized Cultural Politics,* ed. Russ Castronovo and Dana D. Nelson (Durham: Duke University Press, 2002), 368–92, quote at 378.

17. FDR's full sentence resonates uncannily with the present moment: "So, first of all, let me assert my firm belief that the only thing we have to fear is fear itself—nameless, unreasoning, unjustified terror which paralyzes needed efforts to convert retreat into advance." "FDR's First Inaugural Address," http://www.bartleby.com/124/pres49.html.

18. See, for example, the website of paper-clip.com, whose white paper "Terror Threats and Anxiety" has been used by universities, colleges, and businesses all over the country to address post–September 11 mentalities: http://www.paper-clip.com/pdf/anxiety.pdf.

19. These words are misquoted in virtually every history of Hollywood, HUAC, and U.S. anticommunism. The text of the film matters less than the panic generated by the word *share.*

20. "Practice of equality" is Jacques Rancière's definition of justice in *Disagreement.*

21. http://www.indiana.edu/~bodnarje/elvisnts.htm.

22. "Teacher, tender, comrade, wife, / A fellow-farer true through life, / Heart-whole and soul-free / The august father / Gave to me." "My Wife," from Robert Louis Stevenson, *Songs of Travel and Other Verses,* Pennsylvania State University Electronic Classics Series (2000): 17.

23. Ernesto Laclau and Chantal Mouffe, *Hegemony and Socialist Strategy: Towards a Radical Democratic Politics* (London and New York: Verso, 1985). This concept is elaborated usefully in Laclau's "The Death and Resurrection of the Theory of Ideology," *Journal of Political Ideologies* 1, no. 3 (1996): 201–20.

24. Virginia Wright Wexman, *Creating the Couple: Love, Marriage, and Hollywood Performance* (Princeton: Princeton University Press, 1993).

25. I refer here to the tradition now associated with John Rawls and, proximately, Martha Nussbaum. See, for example, John Rawls, *Political Liberalism* (New York: Columbia University Press, 1995), and Martha C. Nussbaum, "Human Functioning and Social Justice: In Defense of Aristotelian Essentialism," *Political Theory* 20 (1992): 202–46.

26. See Charles Baudelaire, "The Painter and Modern Life," for a classic example of the gendering of modernity; also Antonio Gramsci, "Americanism and Fordism," in *An Antonio Gramsci Reader: Selected Writings, 1916–1935,* ed. David Forgacs (New York: Schocken Books, 1988), 286–96. For the keystone contemporary arguments, see Andreas Huyssen, "Mass Culture as Woman: Modernism's Other," in *After the Great Divide: Modernism, Mass Culture, and Postmodernism* (London: Macmillan, 1988); Patrice Petro, "Mass Culture and the

Feminine: The 'Place' of Television in Film Studies," *Cinema Journal* 25, no. 3 (1986): 5–21.

27. Alan Nadel, *Containment Culture* (Durham: Duke University Press, 1997); Michel Foucault, "Governmentality," in *The Foucault Effect: Studies in Governmentality,* ed. Graham Burchell, Colin Gordon, and Peter Miller (Chicago: University of Chicago Press, 1991), 87–104.

28. Michael Rogin, *Intellectuals and McCarthy: The Radical Specter* (Cambridge: MIT Press, 1967); Paul Buhle and David Wagner, *Radical Hollywood: The Untold Story behind America's Favorite Movies* (New York: New Press, 2002); Michael Denning, *The Cultural Front: The Laboring of American Culture in the Twentieth Century* (New York and London: Verso, 1998); Frances Stonor Saunders, *The Cultural Cold War: The CIA and the World of Arts and Letters* (New York: New Press, 1999); Larry May and Elaine Tyler May, eds., *Recasting America: Culture and Politics in the Age of Cold War* (Chicago: University of Chicago Press, 1989); Eric Bentley, ed., *Thirty Years of Treason: Excerpts from Hearings before the House Committee on Un-American Activities, 1938–1968,* introduction by Frank Rich (1971; reprint, New York: Nation Books, 2002).

29. See Lauren Berlant and Michael Warner, "Sex in Public," *Critical Inquiry* 24, no. 2 (1998): 547–66.

30. See Antonio Gramsci, *An Antonio Gramsci Reader,* ed. David Forgacs (New York: Schocken Books, 1988), 246–74.

31. Elaine Hadley, *Melodramatic Tactics: Theatricalized Dissent in the English Marketplace, 1800–1885* (Stanford: Stanford University Press, 1977).

32. See Nadel, *Containment Culture,* for a summary of the place of containment in U.S. aesthetic and political domains.

33. Eli Zaretsky, "The Culture Wars of the 1960s and the Assault on the Presidency: The Meaning of the Clinton Impeachment," in *Our Monica, Ourselves: The Clinton Affair and the National Interest,* ed. Lauren Berlant and Lisa Duggan (New York: New York University Press, 2001), 9–33; see also Denning, *The Cultural Front,* and Gerald Horne, *Class Struggle in Hollywood, 1930–1950: Moguls, Mobsters, Reds, Stars, and Trade Unionists* (Austin: University of Texas Press, 2001).

34. Peter N. Stearns, *American Cool: Constructing a Twentieth Century Emotional Style* (New York: New York University Press, 1994).

35. See, for example, Peter Filene, "Cold War Culture Doesn't Say It All," in *Rethinking Cold War Culture,* ed. Peter J. Kuznick and James Burkhart Gilbert (Washington, DC: Smithsonian Institution Press, 2001), 156–74; Alan Brinkley, "The Illusion of Unity in Cold War Culture," in *Rethinking Cold War Culture,* 61–74.

36. Greg Myers, "Vox Pop Interviews in Media Events," forthcoming.

37. Gilles Deleuze and Félix Guattari, *L'Anti-oedipe. Capitalisme et schizophrénie,* vol. 1 (Paris: Minuit, 1972). Translated by Robert Hurley, Mark Seem, and Helen R. Lane under the title *Anti-Oedipus: Capitalism and Schizophrenia* (Minneapolis: University of Minnesota Press, 1983).

38. Mary Poovey, *A History of the Modern Fact: Problems of Knowledge in the Sciences of Wealth and Society* (Chicago: University of Chicago Press, 1998); Mary

Poovey, *Making a Social Body: British Cultural Formation, 1830–1864* (Chicago: University of Chicago Press, 1995).

39. The ur-text for thinking about time/space compression is David Harvey, *The Condition of Postmodernity: An Inquiry into the Origins of Cultural Change* (London: Blackwell, 1990).

40. Chela Sandoval, *Methodology of the Oppressed* (Minneapolis: University of Minnesota Press, 2000).

41. See, for example, the scandal surrounding a photograph of Anglo-American firemen hoisting a flag near the World Trade Center, which was used as a model for a monument commemorating the heroism of the New York emergency medical personnel and firefighters. When the statue based on it followed the representational norms of liberal multiculturalism, by mixing one Latino and one African American with one Anglo fireman, some mainly Anglo-American pundits were outraged, because the statue then would not be "historically" a true rendering of the photograph, because the NYC fire department is over 90 percent Anglo-American, and because it was deemed condescending, as one website put it, to mobilize "affirmative action . . . for dead people." Counterarguments about inclusiveness were deemed mere whining by these pundits. See the news articles on http://www.september11news.com/FDNY Fireman.htm; http://www.nynewsday.com/news/ny-statue0118,0,6116265 story. The web yields huge numbers of anti-PC, antistatue diatribes from all over the political spectrum: see the archives at instapundit.com and http://www.bigglesguy.pwp.blueyonder.co.uk/nyrev.html, for example.

42. Pierre Bourdieu, *Outline of a Theory of Practice,* trans. Richard Nice (Cambridge: Cambridge University Press, 1972), 96.

Part II

RESPONSES TO DANGER IN STATE & SOCIETY

Containing Dissent

THE WEAKEST LINK? ACADEMIC DISSENT IN THE "WAR ON TERRORISM"

Hugh Gusterson

> Let us not be afraid of debate or dissent—let us encourage it. For if we should ever abandon these basic American traditions in the name of fighting Communism, what would it profit us to win the world when we have lost our soul?
>
> —John F. Kennedy[1]

> America is a trap: its promises and dreams . . . are too much to live up to and too much to escape.
>
> —Greil Marcus[2]

Writing only a week after al Qaeda's destruction of the World Trade Center on September 11, Congressman John Conyers wondered whether the right-wing reaction to the attack might not do more damage to America than the attack itself had done. "Historically," he said, "it has been at times of inflamed passions and national anger that our civil liberties proved to be at greatest risk, and the unpopular group of the moment was subject to prejudice and deprivation of liberty."[3] And indeed, in the months following September 11, Americans saw a dramatic curtailment of their civil liberties by their leaders in Congress and in the White House, while the bandwidth of acceptable debate narrowed perceptibly in the media. For example, the government was given the power to ban organizations it deemed terrorist organizations without judicial review; the government assumed the power to detain foreign citizens indefinitely without charging them with any crime or permitting them to see a lawyer; the government's wiretap powers were extended; racial profiling of Arab Americans was expanded and Arab men resident in the United States were summoned to local INS headquarters for "interviews"; universities were required to provide the government with information on foreign students that would formerly have been treated as confidential; attorney-client privileges were rolled back in cases of suspected terrorism; and the ban on FBI surveillance of political movements within the United States, instituted in the 1970s after revelations about the Cointelpro program of domestic surveillance, was rescinded.

At the same time the free expression of opinion in civil society was subtly constricted. Newspaper editors were instructed to bury mention of civilian casualties caused by U.S. bombing of Afghanistan deep in their stories, while CNN told its reporters always to mention that "the Pentagon has repeatedly stressed that it is trying to minimize civilian casualties in Afghanistan, even as the Taliban regime continues to harbor terrorists who are connected to the September 11 attacks that claimed thousands of innocent lives in the U.S."[4] Bill Maher, host of the late-night ABC show *Politically Incorrect,* lost advertisers—and, eventually, the show itself—after he observed that it was more "cowardly" to fire Cruise missiles from a distance than to fly planes into buildings at the cost of one's own life; and boycott campaigns were launched against such figures as the novelist Barbara Kingsolver and the cartoonist Ted Rall after they spoke against the Bush administration's war on terror.[5] At the more ridiculous end of the spectrum, Yahoo! removed sites containing the word *jihad,* and Clear Channel, owner of 1,200 radio stations across the country, drew up a list of 100 "questionable" songs—including John Lennon's "Imagine"—that disc jockeys were instructed to avoid.[6]

These actions are only the most recent manifestation of a depressing American tradition of repressing dissent in times of crisis. This tradition goes all the way back to the first years of the Republic when John Adams, undeterred by the recent passage of the First Amendment to the Constitution, pushed through the Sedition Act of 1798 making it illegal to say or write anything that would inflame public opinion against Congress or the president at a time when the Republic's new rulers were unnerved by the recent French Revolution and Irish rebellion.

A little over a century later, at another moment when the U.S. government feared the influence of revolutionary ideas from Europe, 900 people were arrested under the Espionage Act for speaking against the draft in World War I. Among those arrested were Emma Goldman and Eugene Debs. Debs told the jury at his trial, "I have been accused of obstructing the war. I admit it. Gentlemen, I abhor war. I would oppose war if I stood alone."[7] The jury gave Debs ten years in prison—a sentence that was upheld by the Supreme Court. Also arrested was pamphleteer Charles Schenck whose conviction was, likewise, unanimously sustained by the Supreme Court in a famous opinion, written by Justice Oliver Wendell Holmes, that likened speaking against the war to the dangerous act of shouting "Fire!" in a crowded theater.[8] Nicholas Murray Butler, president of Columbia University, caught the mood of many at the time when, in his 1917 commencement address at Columbia, defending the firing of professors who opposed World War I, he said:

> What had been tolerated before becomes intolerable now. What had been wrongheadedness was now sedition. What had been folly was now treason. . . . There is and will be no place at Columbia University . . . for any person who opposes or counsels opposition to the effective enforcement of the laws of the United States or who acts, speaks, or writes treason.[9]

Immediately after World War I the U.S. government became increasingly concerned by widespread labor unrest and a wave of radical agitation around the country. Following a series of anarchist bombings, Attorney General Mitchell Palmer sent 500 FBI agents into action (under the command of the twenty-four-year-old J. Edgar Hoover) in the Palmer Raids of 1919–20. Invoking the Immigration Act of 1918 and targeting recent immigrants from Europe (presumed to be radical troublemakers), the government arrested thousands, detaining many for months without trial before deporting them. As part of this campaign, 4,000 were arrested in January 1920.[10]

In the next world war, the U.S. government decided that Japanese Americans—an internal enemy defined by ethnicity—constituted a security threat, and it interned 110,000 of them. Meanwhile many conscientious objectors were used as human guinea pigs by U.S. military doctors in mustard gas and malaria experiments.[11] In the decade after the end of World War II, as the Cold War intensified, communists or suspected communists found themselves the target of the next witchhunt. While Senator Joseph McCarthy was the most visible exponent of the campaign to purge suspected leftists, many liberals acquiesced and participated in a movement that had a chilling effect on dissent and cost many their jobs and reputations. According to one estimate, over 6 million Americans were investigated in some way in the McCarthyist period.[12]

These episodes punctuate a clear historical pattern in times of war and crisis in the United States. In such times, again and again, free speech has been curtailed, while dissident intellectuals, immigrants, and ethnic minorities have been targeted for harassment, deportation, or detention, all without regard to the constitutional niceties that are more carefully observed between these historical eruptions of panic—constitutional guarantees that, incidentally, charter the American exceptionalist ideology in whose name, paradoxically, repression is then carried out. Taking these past incidents as prologue, this essay analyzes a recent modest but interesting attempt to constrict free speech and intimidate critics of government policy in the context of the current war on terrorism. The attempt in question, a new variation on an old American theme, is the effort by the American Council of Trustees and Alumni (ACTA)—a conservative group founded by Lynne Cheney—to blacklist critical voices on campus after September 11.

It is no coincidence that the right targeted dissent on campus after September 11. On the one hand, universities have become profoundly important to the national security state because they train the scientists and engineers who will develop the next generation of weaponry and because they conduct so much military-sponsored research on campus. On the other hand, American universities have become increasingly globalized in recent years, providing environments where American students mingle freely with international students, many of them from countries in Asia or the Middle East regarded with some suspicion by the American national security apparatus. Meanwhile many university faculty, especially those that came of age in the 1960s, are "tenured radicals" who openly espouse liberal political ideas to which their students may be exposed. It is the multiculturalist internationalism of the contemporary American academy and the dissenting political views of some of its faculty that the ACTA report sought to target.

As we shall see, ACTA's attack on the academy largely (though not entirely) failed, and it is instructive to ask how that turned out to be so, as well as what ACTA's failure might tell us about the evolving nature of public discourse on state security and intellectual dissent in the contemporary United States. On the one hand it is encouraging to see that, even after terrorists killed almost 3,000 Americans on their own soil in a single day, there is a protected space in American civil society for dissent against the ensuing war on terrorism and, in particular, that mainstream public commentators recognize and value the importance of vigorous political debate on campus. On the other hand, the terrible suspicion grows that such dissent can be tolerated precisely because it is ornamental to that which it opposes and may even, perversely, serve to legitimate a campaign of American repression abroad by symbolizing tolerance at home. In other words, mainstream defense of dissent on campus may constitute an example of what Herbert Marcuse called "repressive tolerance."[13] Further, the only language in which the dissenters can make their claims to be heard is the betrayed language of America itself—a language that affirms the national project, which, in its instantiation in the war on terror, is precisely what is being opposed. Sacvan Bercovitch, the cultural critic who has explored this general paradox the most closely, argued at the end of his book on moral critiques of America from the seventeenth through the nineteenth centuries that "in every case, the defiant act that might have posed fundamental social alternatives became instead a force against social change."[14] This is because, in the context of American public discourses that have secularized the old biblical jeremiads of the founding Puritans, "to condemn the profane is to express one's faith to a spiritual ideal. To condemn 'false Americans' as profane is to express one's faith in a national ideology. In effect, it is to transform what might have been a search for moral or social alternatives into a call for cultural revitalization."[15]

In order to provide a context for this argument, we must first take a detour through the history of McCarthyism, especially as it relates to the fate of critical academics in the 1940s and 1950s.

THE MCCARTHYIST EXPERIENCE

The end of World War II and the beginning of the Cold War marked the transition in American society to a culture of what has variously been termed permanent war, pure war, or total war.[16] Where earlier wars had been relatively brief in duration and had been premised in their execution and representation upon a clearer distinction between combatants and civilians, by the 1940s the United States found itself in a war that required the total mobilization of society for a global struggle of indefinite duration. This struggle required that the United States maintain wartime levels of military expenditure for decades, that American citizens acquiesce in the mass targeting of civilians characteristic of the nuclear age, and that a robust social consensus endure in favor of the half-century geopolitical duel that Mary Kaldor has called "the imaginary war."[17] Thus was created a permanent war society in which large sectors of the economy were locked into military production and in which a constant state of patriotic arousal among the citizenry became vital. In the words of Vannevar Bush, the MIT dean of engineering who went on to head the federal Office of Scientific Research and Development during World War II, "war is increasingly total war, in which the armed services must be supplemented by active participation of every element of the civilian population."[18]

In a way that is only now beginning to be studied, the entrenchment of permanent war had a transformative effect on all the key institutions in American society: the military, the mass media, the church, and the corporations. I am interested here in its effect on the university.[19] The managers of the postwar national security state had observed that university scientists played a key role in the development of the atomic bomb during World War II, and they realized that the scientific resources of the academy would be vital in the development of new weapons and new knowledge about the enemy during the Cold War. Scientists, and with them the universities, were now a key sinew of war. But the university was also a source of anxiety for national security bureaucrats and their allies; they observed that the scientists' movement against the nuclear arms race was grounded in the universities, and they were, not without reason, apprehensive that the ivory tower of academe sheltered freethinkers who might become foci of opposition to the project of permanent war.[20]

Thus the first decade or so of the Cold War saw the colonization of the university by the national security state in two different ways: through increased funding for military research and through repression of "anti-American" dissent—at least until the progressive backlash of the 1960s and 1970s led to a curtailment of classified research on campus and a partial reclamation of the humanities and social sciences for the production of progressive knowledge. Before that backlash the early years of the Cold War saw a massive influx of government funding into the universities, funneled through the Office of Naval Research and the newly established National Science Foundation,[21] to support research that might have military utility and to produce a massive reserve labor force of potential military scientists. In the words of historian of science David Kaiser, "a Cold War logic emerged, according to which physicists, government bureaucrats, and journalists alike equated the nation's security with the production of young physicists. Most American physicists were not spending the bulk of their time working directly on weapons during the 1950s. Yet they were getting money from defense-related bureaus to keep a constantly expanding body of *potential* weapons-makers in the ranks."[22] This influx of government funding—and with it the magnetic force of the military bureaucrats' research priorities—had most effect on engineering and physics. As Stuart Leslie writes, the research priorities of the defense bureaucrats shaped "our scientific community's diminished capacity to comprehend and manipulate the world for other than military ends," as they nudged the scientists and engineers of such universities as MIT and Stanford toward "a knowledge of microwave electronics and radar systems rather than alternating current theory and electric power networks; of ballistic missiles and inertial guidance rather than commercial aircraft and instrument landing systems; of nuclear reactors, microwave acoustic-delay lines, and high-powered traveling-wave tubes rather than Van de Graaff generators, dielectrics, and X-ray tubes."[23]

While the impact of the Cold War national security state on science and engineering is hard to miss, there was also an effect on the nascent social sciences and on the humanities. As Rebecca Lowen has shown in her fine study of Stanford as "the Cold War University," the ambient noise of McCarthyism and the priorities of the national security state (often mediated through such institutions as the Ford Foundation) reshaped social science departments and journals, often turning them away from an engagement with Marxist theory and ethical issues toward quantitative analyses of public opinion at home and of development politics in those third world societies where the two superpowers were competing for hegemony. This era saw the rise of area studies—for example, at MIT's new Center for International Studies[24] and at Harvard University's new Center for Russian Research—often funded directly or indirectly by the Department of Defense and by the CIA. These national security bureaucrats now funded studies of mind control in psychology departments, for example,[25] and studies of the sources of peasant insurrection in sociology and anthropology departments—including the notorious Phoenix Program of the 1960s. Writing about the effects of this on my own discipline, anthropology, Laura Nader observes that the *Selected Papers of the American Anthropologist* from 1946 to 1970, astonishingly, contain not a single reference to Karl Marx, and that these years saw the rise of the kind of quantitative approaches and area studies in anthropology that were of use to the national security state. Summarizing the effects on anthropology, she writes:

> Our numbers were expanded for Cold War research, our subject matter was channeled and defined by funding agencies, our methodologies were revolutionized by military technology. Leading anthropologists, in the complicitous role of activist Cold Warriors, wittingly participated in or at least condoned formulation of CIA and DoD plans for secret interventions into the internal affairs of sovereign states; [nuclear] testing in the Pacific was condoned by omission. Some anthropologists monitored the loyalty of other anthropologists and our informants, creating a climate of intellectual repression, or at least encouraged intellectual products that fit with the Cold War syndrome.[26]

This sort of disciplining of dissent in the academy became commonplace as the McCarthyists took aim not just at Hollywood scriptwriters and State Department officials, but at academics as well. In fact, roughly 20 percent of the witnesses called by the House Un-American Activities Committee (HUAC) were academics.[27] While Richard Lewontin has written that "the Cold War witch-hunts were the continuation by state legislators and the Congress of a history of attack on radicals by ambitious politicians that began with the Palmer Raids and that was only interrupted briefly by World War II,"[28] I do not believe that we can understand the unique scale and intensity of the McCarthyist purges without situating them in the special context of the hysteria accompanying the accelerating Cold War as the superpowers skirmished over Berlin, went to war in Korea, and embarked on an unprecedented and terrifying nuclear arms race.

In any case, regardless of the precise relationship between

McCarthyism and the Cold War, we can agree that McCarthyism had a devastating effect on the academic left in the 1950s. Hundreds of academics were explicitly targeted by Red hunters, many of them losing their jobs, while, as Ellen Schrecker argues in her superb history of McCarthyism in the universities, many, many more were intimidated by the purges from speaking their minds on the issues of the day, consigning large swathes of the American academy to a bland orthodoxy from which it only emerged in the 1960s.

We might make three observations about the way McCarthyism worked in the academic community in the 1940s and 1950s. First, as Schrecker points out, the genius of McCarthyism lay in its functioning as a two-stage process that decentered responsibility and thus guilt, making the purging of leftists from public life a phenomenon that seemed to happen as much automatically as through the agency of particular individuals. In the first stage of this process suspected communists were publically named by, for example, the House Un-American Activities Committee (HUAC) or through FBI whispering campaigns. While a few of those summoned before HUAC were imprisoned, most were punished not by the state but by employers who fired them once they had been stigmatized in public. As Schrecker puts it, "the bifurcated nature of this process diffused responsibility and made it easier for each participant to dissociate his or her action from the larger whole"[29] since the list makers could say that they were not firing anyone, while the employers could say that they were just protecting their institutions from being tarnished by employees who had become disreputable.

This process, incidentally, bears some resemblance to the functioning of state repression in Eastern Europe in the 1970s and 1980s. Often, dissident intellectuals were not imprisoned—or were only intermittently imprisoned—but were unemployable by the universities and had to work as manual laborers. Václav Havel, reflecting on the nature of communist repression in Czechoslovakia, has pointed out that this system of repression functioned for so many decades precisely because of its decentered nature, and that repression was not so much something the state did to civil society as something society did to itself through the instigation of the state. The two-stage process also bears some resemblance to the functioning of death squads in Latin America and the modus operandi of the radical wing of the antiabortion movement in the United States: one set of people would draw up lists of suspected leftists in Latin America or of abortion doctors in the United States and, once these lists entered circulation, the people on the lists could be targeted by others.

Second, and as an obvious corollary, a lot of the dirty work of McCarthyism was done by those from whom one might have expected better: university trustees, administrators, and even liberal NGOs.[30] In Richard Lewontin's words, "The greatest direct enemy of the left in the academy was not the coherent policy of the state, but the opportunism and cowardice of boards of trustees and university administrators."[31] One could fill a very long book with lamentable examples of this phenomenon, but one (plucked more or less at random) will suffice to illustrate Lewontin's point: in 1952 Senator Pat McCarran summoned the distinguished historian M. I. Finley before his Senate Committee on Internal Security and asked him if he was a communist. He denied being a member of the Party but refused to answer questions about others. A faculty committee at Rutgers University, where Finley taught, investigated and concluded that he had a constitutional right to remain silent as he had done. The Board of Trustees, on the other hand, voted unanimously to fire him. One trustee said of the faculty committee he voted to overrule that it has "treat[ed] this whole thing as an abstract situation in which the niceties of the law . . . are given preeminence. It seems to me that we lost sight of the fact that we are at war with Communism."[32] Rutgers, like so many universities, was following the motto of Yale's president, Charles Seymour: "There will be no witch-hunts at Yale because there will be no witches."[33] University trustees and administrators were concerned that the presence of alleged Reds on their faculties would sully the reputations of their universities, reduce alumni giving to private universities, and excite the hostility of state legislatures toward public universities. In many cases, with what in retrospect can only appear remarkable self-delusion, university trustees and administrators claimed that, in purging their faculties of controversial alleged Reds, they were protecting their universities and thereby safeguarding free speech. In Ellen Schrecker's words:

> At no point did the college teachers, administrators, and trustees who cooperated with McCarthyism by evicting unfriendly witnesses and other suspected Communists from their faculties admit that they were repressing dissent. On the contrary, in their public statements and in the docu-

> mentary record that they produced, they often claimed that they were standing up to McCarthyism and defending free speech and academic freedom. . . . The extraordinary facility with which the academic establishment accommodated itself to the demands of the state may well be the most significant aspect of the academy's response to McCarthyism.[34]

The third lesson of McCarthyism in the academy in the 1940s and 1950s is that, in an atmosphere of moral panic and national emergency, the victims of McCarthyism were abandoned by those institutions outside the academy that might have been expected to defend their academic freedom. I am thinking here in particular of the American Association of University Professors (AAUP) and the Supreme Court. During World War I the AAUP had officially taken the position that it would not defend any professor who engaged in antiwar activity, whether that activity was strictly legal or not.[35] At the beginning of the McCarthyist era the AAUP adopted the more courageous official position that being Communist was not per se grounds for dismissal from an academic post unless the person in question was deceitful about their affiliations or engaged in illegal activity. In practice, however,

> the AAUP, the OSHA of academe [was] delinquent in policing the educational industry during the height of McCarthyism. The organization's stated devotion to the principles of academic freedom remained firm throughout this period. . . . But it did not censure any school which had violated those principles. And it did not even publish any reports about them. . . . The Association's failure to perform its expected function had a profound and devastating effect on the academic profession's efforts to combat McCarthyism and contributed as much, if not more, to the inability of the nation's college teachers to protect their colleagues as the shortcomings of individual professors and faculties.[36]

As for the Supreme Court, as late as 1959, five years after the Senate censured Joe McCarthy, in the *Barenblatt* decision they voted 5–4 that academics could be imprisoned for refusing to answer the question whether they had ever been a Communist.[37]

MCCARTHYISM TODAY: THE AMERICAN COUNCIL OF TRUSTEES AND ALUMNI

I have been arguing that, at the beginning of the Cold War, the university became a focus of desire, interest, and anxiety for an expansive national security state eager to enlist the research resources of the academy for the project of permanent war but nervous about critiques of this project from within the academy. The same has also been the case at the beginning of the war on terrorism. The managers of the national security state have since September 11 let it be known that they are interested in whatever contributions the university might make to the development of, for example, biowarfare detectors, information warfare defenses, airport security technologies, or even Middle Eastern area studies. The government is interested here in such projects as the new Center for Soldier Nanotechnology, financed by a $50 million grant from the army, announced by MIT in March 2002.[38]

On the other hand, the managers of the national security state and their allies are concerned that the university may be a locus of dangerous cultural and ideological instability.[39] They worry that the humanities departments of universities are staffed by "tenured radicals"[40] who came of age in the 1960s and are trying to indoctrinate a new generation of American youth in the pernicious ways of relativism, multiculturalism, and antimilitarism. And they worry that, in the era of globalization, American universities have become among the most globalized of American institutions, having aggressively recruited foreign students and faculty, and that there may be a dangerous structural contradiction between the multinational nature of the country's leading colleges and universities and the state's need to enlist these institutions as key allies in its new permanent war project, the replacement for the misplaced Cold War, namely, the war on terrorism. If the Cold War university sat astride a contradiction between its national security commitments and its commitments to liberal ideals—a contradiction that tore many university communities apart in the 1960s—the emerging university in the age of terrorism and of globalization must deal with a new contradiction between its commitments to national security and to the multiculturalism of a globalized, postcolonial society.

The anxiety that the American university may be a sort of multinational Trojan horse in our midst can be seen in recent initiatives to police foreign students in the United States. The crudest of these initiatives was Senator Dianne Feinstein's proposal, inspired by concern that over half a million foreign students are currently enrolled in U.S. colleges and universities and that future terrorists might be secreted in their midst, to impose a six-month moratorium on student visas.[41] (This proposal was beaten back by intense lobbying from American colleges and universities that rely on foreign students to pay full tuition and thus subsidize the education of American students. At my own university, MIT, for example, foreign students from over one hundred different countries account for 8 percent of our undergraduates and 40 percent of our graduate students.)[42] Meanwhile the presidential science adviser, John Marburger, attempting to revive an old Cold War program of campus surveillance, made a speech after September 11 in which he suggested that foreign students' access to certain sensitive classes and library facilities (in nuclear engineering, for example) might be policed—a proposal completely at odds with the university's self-image as an environment where knowledge and ideas circulate freely. At the same time the Justice Department contacted 220 colleges and universities in the two months after September 11, requesting access to confidential files of students from Middle Eastern countries—or, in some cases, of American students with names that sounded Arabic. Most colleges and universities acceded to the requests for the information on what subjects the students were studying, how they were performing, and where they were living. In some cases, students were summoned for interviews with FBI agents.[43]

These attempts to police the foreign student body were accompanied by reinvigorated attacks by conservative media pundits on an old target—what Helle Bering, writing in the *Washington Times,* called "the rampant suspicion bordering on hatred of everything American that has been nurtured by the academy for decades" and what Kay Hymowitz and Harry Stein call, a little inelegantly, "the blame-America-firsters" in the academy.[44] In a context where the media was reporting that the new generation of students was more patriotic than its predecessors and that the new president of Harvard, Lawrence Summers, was appealing to his colleagues to set aside the legacy of division from the Vietnam War and to show respect for the U.S. military,[45] the right saw an opportunity to renew its old attacks on the campus left. Leading the charge was an organization called the American Council of Trustees and Alumni (ACTA).

Founded in 1995 by Lynne Cheney, ACTA bills itself as "the largest private source of support for higher education." In 2000 it gave away $3.4 billion, much of it raised from conservative foundations such as the John M. Olin Foundation. ACTA's National Council includes such luminaries of the cultural right as the novelist Saul Bellow, the former secretary of education and drug czar William Bennett, the conservative columnist Georgie Anne Geyer, and *New Republic* publisher Martin Peretz. ACTA has sought to attack "political correctness" on campus—affirmative action, multiculturalism, and speech codes—and to encourage the teaching of a patriotically correct version of American history. To that end it has organized conservative trustees and alumni into a powerful and well-connected lobby. Many saw ACTA's influence at work when Governor Jeb Bush of Florida abolished the Board of Trustees of the University of Florida and replaced it with a set of smaller boards staffed largely by conservative politicians and executives; ACTA was given the task of organizing the orientation sessions for the new trustees.[46]

In November 2001 ACTA sent to media all over the country, as well as to 3,000 college and university trustees, a 38-page report entitled *Defending Civilization: How Our Universities Are Failing America and What Can Be Done about It.*[47] Calling American faculty "the weak link in America's response" to the events of September 11, the report notes "a shocking divide between academics and the public at large [as] professors across the country sponsored teach-ins that typically ranged from moral equivocation to explicit condemnations of America. While America's elected officials from both parties and media commentators from across the spectrum condemned the attacks and followed the President in calling evil by its rightful name, many faculty demurred. . . . Some even pointed accusatory fingers, not at the terrorists, but at America itself."[48] Citing "an atmosphere increasingly unfriendly to the free exchange of ideas," the report goes on to claim that students and untenured faculty "are intimidated by professors and fellow students if they question 'politically correct' ideas or fail to conform to a particular ideology."[49] Noting disapprovingly that "universities are rushing to add courses on Islamic and Asian cultures" after September 11, the ACTA report calls instead for more courses on "the unique contributions of America and Western civilization—the civilization under attack" and suggests that, toward that end, "alumni should protest, donors should fund new programs, and trustees should demand action."[50]

The vast bulk of the ACTA report, however, consists of a simple list of 117 patriotically incorrect comments attributed in each case to a faculty member or student identified by name and university affiliation. This caught my attention, since the first quotation in the report is attributed to me—an act of attribution that soon had upstanding American citizens sending me hate mail and media calling from all over the United States and even beyond to inquire about my patriotism.[51]

The list of quotations in the ACTA report is a bizarre compendium. Many make the point that the United States has itself in recent years been responsible, in such places as Guatemala, El Salvador, and Indonesia, for the mass killing of civilians and that the U.S. relationship to terrorism is not only one of victimhood. Although these statements seem to me to be incontrovertibly true, one can see why they annoyed the authors of the ACTA report, Jerry Martin and Anne Neal. Some of the comments quoted in the report I myself find misguided and in poor taste—for example, "I was cheering when the Pentagon got hit. . . . The American flag . . . should be used for toilet paper for all I care."[52] Others are, well, just odd. George Lakoff's phrase (number 8 on the list), "the Pentagon, a vaginal image from the air, penetrated by the plane as missile," reminds me why I sometimes find cultural criticism a little stretched, but the comment is hardly disloyal or unpatriotic. In the case of other quotations on the blacklist it is hard to see why they are deemed offensive, even by the right-wing mind. What, for example, is so offensive about Joel Beinin's sentiment (number 83 on the list) that "if Osama bin Laden is confirmed to be behind the attacks, the United States should bring him before an international tribunal on charges of crimes against humanity"? Or Strobe Talbott's statement (number 36 on the list) that "it is from the desperate, angry, and bereaved that these suicide pilots came"? Neither comment exonerates the attackers of September 11. And, unless triteness is a crime, why do the authors of the ACTA report object to the claim (number 49 on their list) that "ignorance breeds hate"—unless it is because the statement was made by someone with an Arab name?

For some professors the media coverage of the ACTA report had immediately unpleasant consequences. Many faculty named in the report found themselves on the sharp end of unpleasantly vitriolic email messages from complete strangers (usually writing from the safe anonymity of Hotmail, AOL, or Yahoo! accounts). Two professors named in the report had particularly unpleasant experiences. Richard Berthold, a tenured professor of history at the University of New Mexico, was quoted in the report as saying "anyone who can blow up the Pentagon gets my vote." Although he quickly apologized for the comment, he found himself the subject of a hastily organized posttenure review.[53] Robert Jensen, a tenured professor of journalism at the University of Texas, Austin, also quoted in the ACTA report, became the target of a mass phone and mail campaign in Texas dedicated to securing his dismissal from the university. Although he was not fired, he did have to endure his university president, Larry Faulkner, writing a letter to the *Houston Chronicle* in which he described himself as "disgusted" by Robert Jensen's opinions, which he described as "undiluted foolishness."[54] (Jensen's supporters felt that it was an abuse of power for a university president to rebuke one of his own faculty members in the media for an opinion; one colleague, Dan Cloud, told the *Chronicle of Higher Education* that "the faculty [at the University of Texas, Austin] felt there was a very clear message that if you stick your neck out, we will disown you. This was a symbolic casting out of Bob Jensen from our intellectual community.")[55]

To my knowledge, however, the only professor to lose his or her job was Sami Al-Arian, a tenured professor of engineering of Palestinian origin at the University of South Florida, who was not named in the ACTA report but was outed by Fox Television's *O'Reilly Factor* for having many years earlier said "Death to Israel!" at a campus rally and for his association with Middle Eastern NGOs that had been investigated (and cleared, incidentally) by the FBI for possible terrorist associations. After he appeared on *The O'Reilly Factor,* Al-Arian received death threats, while the university received mail from angry alumni insisting he be fired.[56]

In the end, the ACTA report did more damage to its authors than to its intended victims. The mainstream press reacted very negatively to the report, giving generous coverage to complaints that it was "McCarthyist," picking apart the weak research and writing of ACTA's staff, and, interestingly, defending the right to dissent on campus in editorials. Some journalists, targeting not so much the purpose of the report but what we might call errors of execution by its authors, remarked on the report's inclusion of quotations most people would find reasonable and in its mistaken attempt to blacklist faculty who turned out to be above reproach. The *Boston Globe,* for example, pointed out that, although the president of Wesleyan College is named in the report, "he strongly supports the Bush administration's response to the terrorist attacks and . . . an American flag has hung on the door of his house since Sept. 11."[57] Similarly, the *New York Times* reported that New York University professor Todd Gitlin was "surprised" to find himself on the list given that he had "draped an American flag across the balcony of his Manhattan apartment and published an essay denouncing anti-American sentiment abroad." The *Times* quoted Gitlin's biting dismissal of the report as "a record-breaking event in the annals of shoddy scholarship."[58]

The media also strongly defended the right to dissent on a university campus. Alex Beam, in his regular column for the *Boston Globe,* quoted an email message from Christopher Bonn, a member of the public who, in appealing to MIT to fire Noam Chomsky for his criticism of American policy, had said that Chomsky's "right to free speech ends the minute he walks onto your campus as an employee." Beam retorted that "if anything, Chomsky's freedom of speech should increase when he sets foot on a university campus."[59] Meanwhile a *Boston Globe* editorial, condemning the ACTA report's "McCarthyesque list of professors' names and comments," says, "Professors are complaining and getting away with it? Great. It means Americans are not the Taliban. We let people talk." The editorial ends on the rousing note: "Praise the critics and contrarians for teaching this lesson: A free society doesn't just accommodate dissenters; it thrives on them."[60] Similarly, a *New York Times* editorial, calling the ACTA report "repugnant," said: "Wartime is precisely the moment when unpopular views and the role of the university as an open forum for ideas must be most vigorously defended."[61]

Some media commentary took the next rhetorical step and argued that, if free speech is gloriously American, then the attempt to repress it must be un-American. A letter to the editor of the *Boston Globe* from Sigmund Roos, a trustee of Hampshire College, said, "Cheney and the American Council of Trustees and Alumni would be well served to engage in the study of American history and 'founding documents,' which they commend to others. There, they will learn that the founding fathers were not threatened by dissent but embraced it."[62] Alfred Lubrano, writing his regular column for the *Philadelphia Inquirer,* denounced "an unsettling notion that equates patriotism with conformity," referring to this as (quoting David Barash) "the Taliban-ization of America."[63] And Robert Jensen, defending himself against ACTA in an opinion piece, articulated this position most pithily by saying, "Many accuse me of being 'anti-American,' but ironically it is their call to limit political debate that is anti-American . . . those calling for my firing are anti-American to the bone; their patriotism is supremely unpatriotic."[64] Another academic targeted in the ACTA report, Joel Beinin, similarly wrote in an op-ed for the *San Francisco Chronicle* that "those who try to enforce conformity of views in the academy and who condemn critics as traitors have more in common with the Taliban than they do with the founders of our nation."[65]

Meanwhile a solidarity campaign with the targets of the ACTA report had begun in academia. While university administrations largely remained silent, some professional associations—the American Anthropological Association and the Society for Social Studies of Science, for example—passed resolutions condemning the report. More creatively, a letter-writing campaign commenced, partly in response to an appeal from the Tufts University historian Martin Sherwin in the *Nation,* to inundate ACTA with ironic letters from people who were not named in the report but said they should have been. Because of the decentered nature of this writing campaign, it is impossible to know how many people took part, though some sent their letters to the *Nation* for posting on its website. Many of these letters mockingly adopted the tone of confessions in Soviet show trials. For example, Claire Potter, a history professor at Wesleyan University, wrote: "I would like to name my own name. . . . On the day that the United States initiated the bombing of Afghanistan, I attended a peace rally run by our students. With other faculty and students, I walked up to a microphone and announced my name, followed by 'and I am against the war,' as I had been asked to do by the organizers." Cheryl Shurtleff, an art professor at Boise State University, wrote: "I offer my own name . . . to be listed in the ACTA Report. . . . I admit to not only posting a reproduction of Jasper Johns's painting *Three Flags* instead of an American flag on my university office bulletin board, but also placing a peace sign in the window of my home. . . . I have also worn a peace-sign button to class." And Louise Westling of the University of Oregon's English department slyly wrote to ACTA to turn herself in for the subversive act of advising her students "to go out and buy a copy of the Constitution and read it carefully."[66] We will never know how the staff of ACTA reacted to such letters and email messages, or if they even read them, but they did make the point that a broader academic community found the ACTA report offensive, more akin to Soviet-style policing of the academy than to American-style free debate, and that this community was willing to stand up for its beliefs.

The charge of McCarthyism was sticking, and, in this negative media environment, some of ACTA's partisans began to distance themselves from the ACTA report. Thus the *New York Times* published a letter from John Bunzel saying, "As a former university president, at San Jose State, and a member of the American Council of Trustees and Alumni, I dissociate myself from its listing of 117 anti-American statements heard on college campuses and for accusing dozens of scholars and students of unpatriotic behavior since September 11." He added that "a college campus is where one expects to hear outrageous and offensive ideas."[67] Two weeks later the *Nation* published a letter from Senator Joseph Lieberman, often identified as a co-founder of ACTA, to Jerry Martin, the president of ACTA and one of the report's two authors. It read in part:

> I was never given the opportunity to review the *Defending Civilization* report before it was made public. I first learned of it through a call to my office from a reporter in Connecticut about a controversy the report had stirred at Wesleyan University.
>
> If I had been given an advanced copy, I would have objected to its content and methodology and asked you either to revise it or make clear that I had no involvement with it. But because that did not happen, and because I have been incorrectly listed on your website as a co-founder of the council, a number of news accounts and commentaries have associated me with the report and incorrectly asserted or implied that I endorse it.
>
> This letter is meant to set the record straight about my disapproval of this report, which I consider unfair and inconsistent for an organization devoted to promoting academic freedom. To avoid any future confusion, I would ask you to remove any reference to me as a "co-founder" of ACTA from your website or other Council documents. And I would ask that you note in any future public statements that I do not support this specific report.[68]

So radioactive had the report become that even Lynne Cheney distanced herself from it. Her spokeswoman told the *New York Times* that, in the *Times*'s words, "Mrs. Cheney was no longer involved with the Council, which was created in 1995. She added, in a Clintonesque evasion, that Mrs Cheney 'has seen' the report—although has not read it."[69]

Meanwhile the ACTA staff quietly doctored the report on their website. In an act that surely suggests their implicit acceptance of the charge of McCarthyism, or at the very least their awareness that the report had turned into a public relations disaster, they took down the original report and replaced it with a new version in which the quotes were no longer associated with named individuals. My own quote, for example, is now attributed to an unnamed "professor of anthropology" at MIT.[70]

DISCUSSION

We will never know what costs, if any, were incurred by those named on ACTA's blacklist. Even though to my knowledge only one professor (Sami Al-Arian) has been fired for his politics in the war on terrorism, and those of us on the list received a welcome outpouring of support from rank-and-file colleagues, this is not the kind of publicity that university administrators or program officers at foundations tend to welcome for their employees or sponsored researchers, and it is possible that for some on the list the taint of controversy and disloyalty cost them job interviews or those big little things that matter so much in academia: a research grant, an invitation to a conference, or an appointment to a faculty committee.[71] Thus, although *Defending Civilization* turned into a public relations disaster for the American Council of Trustees and Alumni, it may still have had subtly deleterious, and often unknowable, consequences for those named in the report. One also presumes that it had a chilling effect on faculty, particularly junior faculty as yet unprotected by tenure, who were not named in the report and realized that they might become a target of similar campaigns for patriotic correctness in the academy in the future if they were not careful. This was presumably one of ACTA's goals in compiling the list in the first place.

Still, the contrast between the academy's response to the ACTA report in 2001–2 and its earlier response to McCarthyism in the 1940s and 1950s is heartening. McCarthyism partly worked by isolating its victims from colleagues who lived in dread that "guilt by association" would make them too targets for university committees, administrators, or trustees seeking to protect their institutions from controversy. In the case of the ACTA report, most university administrators seem to have taken no action against any faculty named there, while the solidarity campaign by colleagues writing to ask if they too could be named in future reports was an important symbolic gesture in affirming that it would not be easy for the right this time around to create the isolation of the blacklisted that in the 1950s was an important precondition for their further persecution. Taken together with the editorial response of such newspapers as the *New York Times* and the *Boston Globe,* which strongly defended academic freedom of speech even in the midst of the unprecendented sense of emergency occasioned by the World Trade Center attacks, this suggests that "academic freedom" has come of age. It is now a much more securely grounded right than it was when professors were fired for speaking against conscription in World War I or for their presumed association with the Communist Party in the 1940s and 1950s. Even though Robert Jensen was publically rebuked for his views by his university president, that president prefaced his attack with the statement that Jensen's right to accuse the United States of terrorism was protected by academic freedom. As Jensen himself put it, "He said I have a First Amendment right to speak. Okay, that's not news to me—I teach the First Amendment. I knew that, but I'm glad he said it in public. In the Fifties, university presidents were not quite so respectful of the First Amendment."[72]

The power of academic freedom is, ironically, further demonstrated by the fact that the authors of the ACTA report invoked it in their own defense. While the tormentors of academic radicals in earlier times were often explicit in arguing that academics forfeited their rights to free speech in times of national crisis, ACTA made no such argument this time around. The ACTA report itself says that "while professors should be passionately defended in their right to academic freedom, that does not exempt them from criticism,"[73] and, in response to the controversy over the report, Lynne Cheney was quoted as saying that "faculty members have the right to express their opinions freely," but that others "have a right to dispute those opinions when they disagree."[74] In a fascinating rhetorical turn, the ACTA report also mimics the discourse of victimhood pioneered by the left in the speech code debates of the 1980s and 1990s. While some on the left argued in the 1980s and 1990s that speech offensive to women and minorities on campus should be restricted out of deference to these groups' feelings, the ACTA report stated that "students have reported more and more that they are intimidated by professors and fellow students if they question 'politically correct' ideas or fail to conform to a particular ideology."[75]

In some media interviews the authors of the ACTA report even claimed that their own right to free speech was being abridged by those accusing them of McCarthyism and, thus, trying to prevent them from speaking their minds. This argument hits the opponents of ACTA's report in their weak spot: just as conservative critiques of dissent as unpatriotic are vulnerable to the argument that, since the days of the founding fathers, the United States has built its national identity upon the protection of dissent, so left-wing critiques of ACTA for McCarthyism snag upon the paradox that, if free speech is sacrosanct, then even obnoxiously McCarthyist speech has a right to protection. In my own view, while all speech (short of libel or shouting "Fire" in a crowded theater) must be protected, we should also recognize that there is a considerable difference between engaging in debate with those one opposes and smearing them by mailing blacklists of their names to the media. If the views of progressive academics are so self-evidently wrong, then it should be easy enough to demonstrate this through reasoned argument. ACTA's resort to ungarnished epithets of indignation, to the rhetoric of ridicule, and to the intimidation of the blacklist as a substitute for intellectual argument—the most offensive response possible to serious academics who live by ideas—suggests a certain intellectual insecurity on their part. While the same norms that enshrine my right to dissent also protect their right to take the low road, it is entirely appropriate to point out that ACTA has been using its right to free speech in an attempt to undermine its opponents' enjoyment of the same right and to remind people that, while speech is free, speech acts can impose a cost on their victims—or, if they seem ill judged, on their authors.

While the moral of this story might seem to be, in line with the Whig interpretation of American history, that academic freedom is safe and that the right to dissent is stronger than ever in the United States, I find myself less optimistic. For one thing, the consolidation of civil liberties and free speech for the few of us who inhabit universities does not necessarily translate into a broader consolidation of civil liberties in the contemporary United States. Even as the mainstream media were defending my right to dissent on campus, they were largely ignoring the Bush administration's suspension of habeas corpus and its attack on ancient legal rights enshrined in the Anglo-American tradition as the administration moved over a thousand foreign residents of the United States into indefinite detention, suspended its adherence to the Geneva Conventions in its treatment of captured prisoners in Afghanistan, and prepared to replace civilian courts, with their guarantees of due process, with military tribunals for those accused of terrorism. I am convinced that future historians will judge us harshly, asking how we could sleep as vital constitutional protections were destroyed, just as we now ask how Americans in World War II could have acquiesced in the mass internment of Japanese Americans. The unavoidable conclusion they will reach is that, if those deprived of their liberties had Arabic names, we did not care what was done to them and did not regard their rights as indivisible from our own, even if they shopped at the same stores as we did, sent their children to the same schools as ours, and lived next door.

There are other limitations to the victory over ACTA. For a start, it is unclear that the opinions attacked in ACTA's report are any closer to being heard now than they were before the controversy. That is because we have been incited to a discourse about the right to dissent that has distracted us from hearing the content of dissenting opinions. As Michelle Chihara puts it, "In the current climate, what is being debated is not the validity of dissenting opinions, but whether dissenting opinions have the right to be heard."[76] Paradoxically, while the public debate over the ACTA report established the right of dissenters on campus to speak, the noise generated by the debate prevented them from being heard so that the outcome is the same as that sought by the McCarthyists—marginalization of the content of dissenting views—but in an environment where, meanwhile, we congratulate ourselves for protecting dissenting views in the academy.

There is, in other words, the danger that dissent functions mainly to legitimate that against which it is cast. The professors dissent in their ivory towers, assuring us through their wordy speeches and articles (like this one) that we live in a free and fair society, and in the meantime we get on with our work of bombing innocent Afghan and Iraqi civilians, locking prisoners of war in Caribbean cages in violation of international law, and detaining those with last names and passports that displease our totalitarian attorney general. I note that the dictionary definition of *dissent* is "a justice's nonconcurrence with the opinion of the majority" or "a religious nonconformity."[77] There is here, surely, a suggestion that dissent is always already doomed as the noble gesture, tolerated but useless, of the minority or the deviant.

Finally, there is the price paid in the insistence that dissent is patriotic. The secret tribute here paid by critique to that which it attacks allows the discourse of patriotism to close the circle, subsuming everything in its path. Dissenters make a powerful rhetorical move in insisting that dissent is an authentically American tradition, and this article has demonstrated the power of the move in the battle for position with ACTA, but the hidden cost of this strategy is the reaffirmation of American sanctimony and of an old dualism between good and bad Americans. In his book *The American Jeremiad,* Sacvan Bercovitch points out that the secularized Puritan discourses of American public life, revolving around America's drama of heeding God's call, make America almost impossible to critique since every instance of political sin gets reincorporated and redeemed into a rhetoric of redemption for a nation in search of its special calling. In Bercovitch's own words, "The Puritans' cries of declension and doom were part of a strategy to revitalize the errand," and "the search for meaning is at once endless and self-enclosed."[78] This is another way in which dissent can function to legitimate that which it opposes. Until Americans can learn to see past the rhetoric of American exceptionalism that unites many dissenters with their opponents, dissent will remain trapped within its role as an ornament of hegemony.

NOTES

1. Quoted in Cathy Malcomb, "American Civil Liberties Derailing: A View from a Train," *Ethical Humanist* (June 2002): 6.

2. Greil Marcus, *Mystery Train: The Image of America in Rock 'n Roll* (New York: Dutton, 1975), 22.

3. John Conyers, "Liberty at Risk," *Washington Post,* September 19, 2001, A33. For an elaboration of Conyers's argument about a historical pattern of abusing civil liberties in times of war and crisis, see Michael Linfield, *Freedom under Fire: U.S. Civil Liberties in Times of War* (Boston: South End Press, 1990).

4. Memo by CNN's Rick Davis, quoted in Howard Kurtz, "CNN Chief Orders 'Balance' in War News," *Washington Post,* October 31, 2001, C1; Robert

Fisk, "Hypocrisy, Hatred, and the War on Terror," *Independent,* November 8, 2001. See also "Fox: Civilian Casualties Not News," press release by Fairness and Accuracy in Reporting, November 8, 2001.

5. Deborah Orin, *New York Post,* September 27, 2001; Carter and Barringer, "A Nation Challenged: Speech and Expression; In Patriotic Time, Dissent Is Muted," *New York Times,* September 28, 2001, A1. Bill Maher said, "We have been the cowards, lobbing Cruise missiles from 2,000 miles away—that's cowardly." For the full text of the article that got Barbara Kingsolver in trouble, see Kingsolver's "And Our Flag Was Still There," *San Francisco Chronicle,* September 25, 2001.

6. *Daily Bruin online,* October 4, 2001; "Chilling Effects of Anti-Terrorism," press release by Electronic Frontier Foundation, November 12, 2001, http://eff.org/Censorship/Terrorism_militias/antiterrorism_chill.html.

7. Howard Zinn, *A People's History of the United States, 1492 to the Present* (New York: HarperCollins, 2003), 367–68.

8. Holmes, delineating the limits to free speech, said, "The question in every case is whether the words used are used in such circumstances and are of such a nature as to create a clear and present danger that they will bring about the substantive evils that Congress has a right to prevent." Quoted in Ellen Schrecker, *Many Are the Crimes: McCarthyism in America* (Boston: Little, Brown, 1998), 61.

9. Quoted in Ellen W. Schrecker, *No Ivory Tower: McCarthyism and the Universities* (New York: Oxford University Press, 1986), 20. On the arrests of Debs and Schenk, see Zinn, *People's History,* 367–69.

10. Zinn, *People's History,* 374–76; Schrecker, *Many Are the Crimes,* 56–59; Clancy Sigal, "John Ashcroft's Palmer Raids," *New York Times,* March 13, 2002, A27.

11. Jonathan Moreno, *Undue Risk: Secret State Experiments on Humans* (New York: W. H. Freeman, 2000), 26, 33.

12. Douglas Miller and Marion Nowak, *The Fifties: The Way We Really Were* (New York: Doubleday, 1977), quoted in Zinn, *People's History,* 429.

13. Herbert Marcuse, "Repressive Tolerance," in *A Critique of Pure Tolerance,* ed. R. P. Wolff, Barrington Moore, and Herbert Marcuse (Boston: Beacon Press, 1969).

14. Sacvan Bercovitch, *The American Jeremiad* (Madison: University of Wisconsin Press, 1978), 204.

15. Bercovitch, *The American Jeremiad,* 179.

16. See Paul Edwards, *The Closed World* (Cambridge: MIT Press, 1996); Chris Gray, *Postmodern War: The New Politics of Conflict* (New York: Guilford Press, 1997); Michael Klare, *War without End: American Planning for the Next Vietnams* (New York: Knopf, 1972); Seymour Melman, *The Permanent War Economy: American Capitalism in Decline* (New York: Touchstone Books, 1974); E. P. Thompson, "Notes on Exterminism, the Last Stage of Civilization," in *Exterminism and Cold War,* ed. New Left Review (London: Verso Books, 1982), 1–34; and Paul Virilio and Sylvere Lotringer, *Pure War* (New York: Semiotext(e), 1983).

17. Mary Kaldor, *The Imaginary War: Understanding the East-West Conflict* (Cambridge, MA: Basil Blackwell, 1990).

18. Vannevar Bush, *Science: The Endless Frontier* (Washington, DC: U.S. Government Printing Office, 1945), 12.

19. For more on this, see Noam Chomsky et al., eds., *The Cold War and the University: Toward an Intellectual History of the Postwar Years* (New York: New Press, 1997); Stuart Leslie, *The Cold War and American Science: The Military-Industrial-Academic Complex at MIT and Stanford* (New York: Columbia University Press, 1993); and Rebecca Lowen, *Creating the Cold War University: The Transformation of Stanford* (Berkeley: University of California Press, 1997).

20. On the scientists' movement against nuclear weapons immediately after World War II, see Alice Kimball Smith, *A Peril and a Hope: The Scientists' Movement in America, 1945–47* (Chicago: University of Chicago Press, 1965), and Jessica Wang, *American Science in an Age of Anxiety: Scientists, Anticommunism, and the Cold War* (Chapel Hill: University of North Carolina Press, 1999).

21. The National Science Foundation saw its budget increase from $100,000 in 1950, the year it was established, to $100 million a decade later. Of this money, 85 percent went to universities (R. C. Lewontin, "The Cold War and the Transformation of the Academy," in *The Cold War and the University*, ed. Noam Chomsky et al., 1–34, 16).

22. David Kaiser, "Putting the 'Big' in 'Big Science': Cold War Requisitions, Scientific Manpower, and the Production of American Physicists after World War II." Paper presented at 25th anniversary of MIT's Program on Science, Technology and Society, 2001, 3–4.

23. Stuart Leslie, *The Cold War and American Science* (Cambridge, MA: MIT Press, 1993), 9.

24. See Donald Blackmer, *The MIT Center for International Studies: The Founding Years, 1951–1969* (Cambridge, MA: MIT Center for International Studies, 2002).

25. For a fascinating study of the CIA's covert funding of psychological research into hallucinogenic drugs and other technologies of mind control in the 1950s, see John Marks, *The Search for the Manchurian Candidate: The CIA and Mind Control* (New York: Norton, 1991). See also Anne Collins, *In the Sleep Room: The Story of the CIA Brainwashing Experiments in Canada* (Toronto: Key Porter Books, 1988).

26. Laura Nader, "The Phantom Factor: Impact of the Cold War on Anthropology," in *The Cold War and the University*, ed. Noam Chomsky et al., 107–46, quote at 139–40. See also Eric Wakin, *Anthropology Goes to War: Professional Ethics and Counterinsurgency in Thailand* (Madison: University of Wisconsin Center for Southeast Asian Studies Monograph 7, 1992); David Price, "Cold War Anthropology: Collaborators and Victims of the National Security State," *Identities* 4, no. 3–4 (1989): 389–430; David Price, "Anthropologists as Spies," *Nation* 271, no. 16 (November 20, 2000): 24–27; and the special issue of *Social Studies of Science*, "Science in the Cold War," especially Mark Solovey, "Project Camelot at the 1960s Epistemological Revolution," *Social Studies of Science* 31, no. 2 (2001): 171–206.

27. Schrecker, *No Ivory Tower,* 10.
28. Lewontin, "The Cold War," 18.
29. Schrecker, *No Ivory Tower,* 9.
30. In her study of scientists in the immediate postwar years Jessica Wang shows that moderate leaders of the Federation of American Scientists (FAS), concerned that the organization was vulnerable to Red-baiting for its work in opposition to the arms race, informed to the FBI on suspected communist colleagues and in some cases ensured their dismissal or, failing that, marginalization within the organization. See Jessica Wang, *American Science in an Age of Anxiety: Scientists, Anticommunism, and the Cold War* (Chapel Hill: University of North Carolina Press, 1999).
31. Lewontin, "The Cold War," 20.
32. Howard Zinn, "The Politics of History in the Era of the Cold War," 41. In *The Cold War and the University,* ed. Noam Chomsky et al., 35–72.
33. Quoted in David Montgomery, introduction, *The Cold War and the University,* ed. Noam Chomsky et al., xi–xxxvii, quote at xx.
34. Schrecker, *No Ivory Tower,* 10, 340.
35. Schrecker, *No Ivory Tower,* 21. When William Schaper, the chair of the University of Minnesota's political science department, was fired in 1917 for opposing the war, the AAUP investigated but did not intervene on his behalf.
36. Schrecker, *No Ivory Tower,* 314–15.
37. Schrecker, *No Ivory Tower,* 3–4.
38. "Army Selects MIT for $50 Million Institute to Use Nanomaterials to Clothe, Equip Soldiers," MIT press release, March 13, 2002; http://web.mit.edu/newsoffice/nr/2002/isn.html.
39. Writing in the *Washington Times,* the conservative columnist Helle Bering observed that according to a September 25, 2001, opinion poll "92 percent of the American people thought the United States should take military action even if casualties occur. By comparison 28 percent of the students at Harvard agreed." Helle Bering, "American Academics Get it Wrong, Again," *Washington Times,* November 28, 2001.
40. See Roger Kimball, *Tenured Radicals: How Politics Has Corrupted Our Higher Education* (New York: HarperCollins, 1990).
41. Sara Hebel and Ron Southwick, "Senator Feinstein May Propose a 6-month Moratorium on Student Visas," *Chronicle of Higher Education,* September 24, 2001.
42. Tanya Schevitz, "Visa Proposal Worries Colleges," *San Francisco Chronicle,* September 29, 2001, A4; Robert J. Sales, "Vest Reaffirms MIT Support for Open Access for International Students at Faculty Meeting," *Tech Talk,* May 22, 2002, 3; MIT, *MIT Facts* (2002), 31.
43. Jacques Steinberg, "In Sweeping Canvasses, U.S. Checks on Mideast Students," *New York Times,* November 12, 2001; Terri Hardy, "FBI Going after College Students' Files," *Sacramento Bee,* September 27, 2001.
44. Helle Bering, "American Academics Get It Wrong, Again"; Kay Hymowitz and Harry Stein, "Earth to Ivory Tower: Get Real!" *City Journal* 11, no. 4 (autumn 2001): 90–101.

45. Patrick Healy, "Harvard Head Urges a Deeper Patriotism," *Boston Globe,* November 25, 2001, A1.

46. Bill Berkowitz, "Lynne Cheney's Campus Crusade," *Working for Change,* November 19, 2001. Berkowitz claims that ACTA was co-founded by Senator Joe Lieberman, but Lieberman himself denied this in a letter sent to the president of ACTA and reprinted in the *Nation.* It was, incidentally, one of the newly constituted boards of trustees of the University of Florida system that took the decision to fire Sami Al-Arian, the tenured professor of engineering at the University of South Florida, after he attracted the ire of Fox Television.

47. ACTA posts the report on its website at http://www.goacta.org/Reports/defciv.pdf . However, the report currently posted there is not the original version. After considerable negative media coverage, ACTA quietly doctored the original report, removing all reference to individual professors. The original report could, at the time of writing, be found archived at http://www.eecs.harvard.edu/~aaron/defciv.pdf. All page references here are to the unexpurgated version of the report. ACTA's distribution of the report is discussed in Emily Eakin, "An Organization on the Lookout for Patriotic Incorrectness," *New York Times,* November 24, 2001.

48. *Defending Civilization,* 1.

49. *Defending Civilization,* 5.

50. *Defending Civilization,* 6–7.

51. The quote attributed to me in the ACTA report is as follows: "Imagine the real suffering and grief of people in other countries. The best way to begin a war on terrorism might be to look in the mirror" (2, 13). These words are accurately quoted from my speech at an MIT campus peace rally, though the quote is taken out of context. (Immediately before the beginning of the quote, I appealed to the audience to imagine the pain and suffering of the people who died in the World Trade Center bombing, asking them afterward to imagine the same suffering inflicted on others abroad if the United States went to war in retaliation for the attacks.)

52. *Defending Civilization,* 12.

53. In a fascinating twist, one of the authors of the ACTA report told a foreign journalist that ACTA opposed firing Richard Berthold for his remark (Duncan Campbell, "Conservative 'Patriots' Target Liberal Academics," *Guardian,* December 19, 2001).

54. Robin Wilson and Ana Marie Cox, "Terrorist Attacks Put Academic Freedom to the Test," *Chronicle of Higher Education,* October 5, 2001; Lee Nichols, "War of Words, " *Austin Chronicle,* September 28, 2001. The quote attributed to Jensen in the ACTA report was that the attacks of September 11 were "no more despicable than the massive acts of terrorism . . . that the U.S. has committed during my lifetime."

55. Wilson and Cox, "Terrorist Attacks."

56. Al-Arian's case has attracted considerable media coverage. See Alex Lynch, "Naked from Sin: The Ordeal of Nahla and Sami Al-Arian," *Counterpunch,* February 25, 2002; Stephen Buckley, "The Al-Arian Argument," *St. Petersburg Times,* March 3, 2002; Rochelle Renford, "Out of the Mouth of Gen-

shaft," *Weekly Planet* (Tampa), February 27, 2002; Graham Brink, "Amid New Probe, Al-Arian Speaks, " *St. Petersburg Times,* February 23, 2002; Barry Klein and Dong-Phuong Nguyen, "Professor Suspended after TV Appearance," *St. Petersburg Times,* September 29, 2001; and "Protecting Free Speech on Campus," *New York Times* editorial, January 27, 2002, 12. Al-Arian had been investigated but never prosecuted by Janet Reno's Justice Department. John Ashcroft's Justice Department reopened the investigation and arrested Al-Arian, who has yet to be tried at the time of writing.

57. Patrick Healy, "Conservatives Denounce Dissent," *Boston Globe,* November 13, 2001. The quotation by Wesleyan's president reads: "Disparities and injustices are there, all the more intolerable because they are embedded in some of the most fundamental aspects of our society and the world we live in. Addressing these disparities and injustices will not be possible if the world community continues to block its own progress and destroy its people in conflicts generated by prejudice and hatred. In this time of crisis, we have an unusual opportunity to see past stereotypes, identify and diminish our own prejudices, and experience a complex world through the sensitivities of others." *Defending Civilization,* 17, quote 38.

58. Eakin, "An Organization on the Lookout for Patriotic Incorrectness."

59. Alex Beam, "Even if Talk's Cheap, Speech Is Still Free," *Boston Globe,* November 13, 2001.

60. "Up with Dissent," *Boston Globe,* November 20, 2001.

61. "Protecting Free Speech on Campus," *New York Times,* January 27, 2002, 12.

62. Sigmund Roos, "Letter to the Editor," *Boston Globe,* November 18, 2001.

63. Alfred Lubrano, "Flaunting Patriotism of a Nasty Stripe," *Philadelphia Inquirer,* November 27, 2001.

64. Robert Jensen, "The 'Patriotic Attack' on Democracy and Higher Education," *Common Dreams,* October 22, 2001.

65. Joel Beinin, "An Obligation to Question Prevailing Wisdom," *Los Angeles Times,* December 30, 2001.

66. These testimonies, collected under the heading "Tattletales for an Open Society," can be found at www.thenation.com/doc.mhtml?i=20020121&c=1&s=tattle20020110.

67. John Bunzel, "Letter to the Editor," *New York Times,* December 6, 2001.

68. Joe Lieberman, "Letter to ACTA," *Nation,* December 18, 2001.

69. Eakin, "An Organization on the Lookout for Patriotic Incorrectness."

70. Some journalists were a little slow on the uptake here. Writing in the *Washington Times,* Helle Bering rebutted allegations that the ACTA report was McCarthyist by saying, "The fact is that none of the folks who made the statements are actually named in the report." Helle Bering, "American Academics Get It Wrong, Again." Ronald Radosh makes perhaps the most amusing comment—amusing because it unwittingly reveals his ignorance in the midst of an opinion piece written in a tone for which the word *arrogant* would be too understated a description. Radosh says "if there is any quarrel I have with ACTA's report, it is their failure to identify by name those whose words they

quote." Ronald Radosh, "Political Correctness, the Academy and the *New York Times*," *FrontPage Magazine*, November 29, 2001.

71. Along these lines, Philip Gasper referred to "the worry that if you speak out you will perhaps lose funding opportunities." Duncan Campbell, "Conservative 'Patriots' Target Liberal Academics," *Guardian*, December 19, 2001.

72. Quoted in Lee Nichols, "War of Words," *Austin Chronicle*, September 28, 2001.

73. *Defending Civilization*, 5.

74. Quoted in Eakin, "An Organization on the Lookout for Patriotic Incorrectness."

75. *Defending Civilization*, 5.

76. Michelle Chihara, "The Silence on Terrorism," *AlterNet*, December 26, 2001.

77. Merriam-Webster online dictionary.

78. Bercovitch, *The American Jeremiad*, xiv, 178.

THE NEW MCCARTHYISM: REPEATING HISTORY IN THE WAR ON TERRORISM

David Cole

The idea of progress is a powerful one. In 1958, in the midst of the Cold War, Yale law professor Ralph Brown opened his comprehensive study of the federal government's loyalty and security program by claiming that censorship, "a traditional device for curbing dangerous speech, . . . is worthy of mention chiefly because, in the political sphere, the times have passed it by."[1] Similarly, as we have launched a war on terrorism in response to the attacks of September 11, 2001, scholars, government officials, and pundits remind us repeatedly that we have avoided the mistakes of the past: we have not locked up people for merely speaking out against the war, as we did during World War I; we have not interned people based solely on their racial identity, as we did during World War II; and we have not punished people for membership in proscribed groups, as we did during the Cold War.[2] But we should be careful about too quickly congratulating ourselves. As Brown went on to argue, "The decline of conventional censorship has been more than offset by a new development, censorship of the speaker rather than the speech."[3] The Cold War did most of its damage by targeting people not for their speech, but for their associations. Similarly, while many argue that we have avoided the mistakes of the past in this crisis, it would be more accurate to say that we have adapted the mistakes of the past, substituting new forms of political repression for old ones.

Today's war on terrorism has already demonstrated our government's remarkable ability to evolve its tactics in ways that allow it simultaneously to repeat history and to insist that it is not repeating history. We have not, it is true, interned people solely for their race, but we have detained over five thousand people in the United States, mostly through administrative rather than criminal procedures, and largely because of their ethnic identity. We have subjected Arab and Muslim noncitizens to discriminatory deportation, detention, registration, fingerprinting, visa processing, and interviews based on little more than their country of origin.[4] We have not, it is true, made it a crime to be a member of a terrorist group, but we have made guilt by association the linchpin of the war's strategy, penalizing people under criminal and immigration laws for providing "material support" to politically selected "terrorist" groups, without regard to whether an individual's support was intended to further or in fact furthered any terrorist activity.

In short, just as it did in the McCarthy era, the government has offset the decline of traditional forms of repression with the development of new forms of repression. A historical comparison reveals not so much a repudiation as an evolution of political repression.

I do not mean to suggest that the Cold War and today's war on terrorism are in all respects identical. History never repeats itself in that literal a sense. For one thing, fear of ideas played a much larger role in the Cold War. Our concerns today stem more from the fear of catastrophic violence made possible by weapons of mass destruction and an enemy that appears immune to deterrence. We who witnessed the World Trade Center towers burn and fall will never forget the horrors of that day. But it is too easy in hindsight to minimize the threat that the nation felt during the Cold War. Then, we were threatened not by a terrorist gang of a few thousand men but by the second largest superpower in the world. Now we speculate about whether the enemy might gain access to weapons of mass destruction. Then, we knew that there were thousands of nuclear bombs trained on our cities. Many of us have nightmares of terrorist attacks today, but at least as many had nightmares then of a nuclear Armageddon.[5] In short, both periods unquestionably were times of mass fear.

As John Lord O'Brian argued in the midst of the Cold War, great fear inevitably produces calls for "preventive" law enforcement; we seek not merely to punish perpetrators after the fact but to prevent the next disaster from occurring.[6] Attorney General John Ashcroft has proudly proclaimed the "preventive" features of his campaign against terrorism. But preventive justice and criminal law are not an easy mix; the fact that the criminal sanction requires the commission of a crime and insists on a strong presumption of innocence until guilt is proven beyond a reasonable doubt makes criminal law an unwieldy mechanism for prevention. Prevention is not of course impossible to achieve through the criminal process. In theory, deterrence operates to prevent crimes, although deterrence is not very realistic when perpetrators are willing to sacrifice their own lives. And the crimes of conspiracy and attempts mean that we do not have to wait for the bomb to explode before arresting individuals and invoking criminal sanctions. Sheikh Omar Abdel Rahman is currently serving multiple life sentences for his role in planning to bomb the tunnels and bridges around Manhattan—the bombs never went off, yet we were able to prosecute the planners on conspiracy charges and incarcerate them for the rest of their lives.[7]

Still, the criminal process, with its rights to counsel, confrontation of adverse witnesses, public trial, and the presumption of innocence, undoubtedly makes preventive law enforcement more difficult. Accordingly, in times of fear, government often looks for ways to engage in prevention without being subject to the ordinary rigors of the criminal process. This essay will argue that the government has invoked two methods in particular in virtually every time of fear. The first, discussed in section I, involves a substantive expansion of the terms of responsibility. Authorities then use these expanded laws to target individuals not for what they do or have done but based on predictions about what they might do. These predictions often rely on the individuals' skin color, nationality, or political and religious associations. The second method, the subject of section II, is procedural—the government invokes administrative processes to control, precisely so that it can avoid the guarantees associated with the criminal process. In hindsight, these responses are virtually always considered mistakes. They invite excesses and abuses, as many innocents suffer—often without any evident gain in security. And most significantly, they compromise our most basic principles—commitments to equal treatment, political freedoms, individualized justice, and the rule of law.

In the current war on terrorism, just as in prior times of fear, our government has adopted both substantive and procedural shortcuts toward the end of preventive justice. While it has altered slightly the tactics of prevention to avoid literally repeating history, in its basic approach the government today is replaying the mistakes of the past. We have learned from history how to mask the repetition, not how to avoid the mistakes.

I. A ROSE BY ANY OTHER NAME—SUBVERSIVE SPEECH, GUILT BY ASSOCIATION, & MATERIAL SUPPORT

The most direct way to authorize preventive law enforcement is to redefine liability broadly so that authorities can sweep up large numbers of people without having to prove that individuals have engaged in specific harmful conduct. In our history, this has been accomplished in two principal ways—by targeting people for their speech and for their associations. In today's war on terrorism, liability has been redefined by penalizing people for providing "material support" to proscribed groups.

Censoring Subversive Speech

In the beginning, we targeted the word. In World War I, Congress made it a crime to utter "any disloyal, profane, scurrilous, or abusive language . . . as regards the form of government of the United States, or the Constitution, or the flag."[8] Over two thousand persons were prosecuted, essentially for speaking out against the war.[9] The Supreme Court affirmed the Sedition Act's constitutionality in a handful of cases at war's end.[10] Few groups or individuals criticized this state of affairs. When Harvard Law Professor Zechariah Chafee did so, Harvard brought him up on charges of being unfit to be a professor. He was acquitted, but only by the narrowest of margins, six to five. It was later revealed that the Justice Department had helped prepare the charges against Professor Chafee.[11]

Today, by contrast, no law criminalizes speaking out against the war; plenty of people have done so, and, with rare exceptions, few have been punished for it. Sami Al-Arian, a tenured computer science professor at the University of South Florida (USF), was one such exception. Shortly after September 11, Professor Al-Arian appeared on Fox Television's *The O'Reilly Factor*, and the program took the occasion to air clips from speeches Professor Al-Arian had made at off-campus pro-Palestinian rallies during the late 1980s in which he chanted, "Death to Israel." When the show aired, USF and Professor Al-Arian received a number of threatening calls. Some threatened violence against Al-Arian; others, no doubt, asked why the university was maintaining on its payroll someone with such extreme views. The governor himself weighed in against Al-Arian. The university suspended the professor and threatened to terminate him, maintaining that his off-campus statements, together with the difficulty of protecting him and his students from threats sparked by the reporting of the statements, warranted dismissal.[12] The issue of suspension for speech was largely superceded in February 2003, when the federal government indicted Al-Arian for allegedly supporting a terrorist organization.

But the most remarkable thing about the Al-Arian case was how atypical it was. In stark contrast to their performance during the Cold War, universities generally have been tolerant of dissenting voices. The American Association of University Professors threatened to censure USF for its suspension of Professor Al-Arian, even after Al-Arian had been indicted.[13] Right-wing organizations have been roundly criticized when they have suggested the need to monitor campuses for antipatriotic teaching and activity, as Hugh Gusterson demonstrates in his account of the reaction to the American Association of Trustees and Alumni's November 2001 report, *Defending Civilization: How Our Universities Are Failing America and What Can Be Done about It*.[14] Similarly, when Attorney General John Ashcroft told Congress that those who faulted him on civil liberties grounds were aiding the enemy, his comments, too, were quickly and broadly condemned.[15] Newspapers, scholars, activists, and human rights and civil rights organizations across the country have openly criticized the administration's response to the September 11 attacks and for the most part have not suffered for doing so. This should not come as much of a surprise. Already in the 1950s, as Professor Brown reported, traditional political censorship seemed to be on the way out. But as censorship of ideas fell into disrepute, the government simply shifted tactics, substituting guilt by association for punishment of speech.

Guilt by Association

In the Cold War, most "radicals" were punished not for their speech but for their membership, affiliation, or sympathetic association with the

Communist Party. This did not mean that people were free to speak, of course, because speech was often used as evidence of one's connection to or sympathy for the Communist Party.[16] But the government could claim that it was avoiding the mistakes of World War I censorship, even as it was effectively suppressing political dissent by targeting communist associations and sweeping a wide swath of progressive political groups under the "communist" label. In November 1950, for example, the attorney general had placed nearly two hundred groups on a list of communist and other subversive organizations, affiliation with which could lead to such consequences as losing a job or being called before the House Un-American Activities Committee (HUAC).[17]

In terms of their effects, guilt by association and censorship of subversive speech are remarkably similar. From the public's vantage point, they demarcate certain political positions as off-limits and dangerous. And because what is proscribed is nearly always defined in open-ended terms and by inscrutable processes, both censorship and guilt by association have an even wider chilling effect, making members of the public leery of engaging in any political activity that might potentially fall within the zone of condemnation. From the government's perspective, both tactics facilitate preventive law enforcement. In World War I, antiwar protesters could be silenced and suppressed before their words were translated into action. Similarly, if the government can target people for their associations, it can disrupt the organization of movements that might someday lead to criminal activity, without having to prove that particular individuals intended further illegal activity of any kind. The Communist Party never actually took any concrete steps to overthrow the U.S. government by force or violence, but because its rhetoric was interpreted as so advocating, the government was able to control and ultimately decimate the Party through guilt by association.

Today, of course, the punishment of dissent during World War I and of political association during the Cold War is seen as a grave error. The Supreme Court, to its credit (although largely after the fact), has developed constitutional doctrines that make these specific mistakes difficult to repeat. On the question of subversive speech, the Court first drew an important line between abstract advocacy and advocacy of illegal conduct in 1957, thereby ending prosecution of Communists for their group's advocacy.[18] In 1969, the Court further developed the test in *Brandenburg v. Ohio*,[19] barring prosecution for speech unless the government shows that the speech was intended and likely to produce imminent illegal conduct, a test that for all practical purposes requires proof of an actual conspiracy to engage in criminal conduct.

In a series of cases beginning as the Cold War was winding down, the Supreme Court also prohibited guilt by association, ultimately declaring it to be "alien to the traditions of a free society and to the First Amendment itself."[20] The prohibition had its genesis in *Scales v. United States*,[21] which effectively ended prosecutions for Communist Party membership under the Smith Act. As the Court stated:

> In our jurisprudence guilt is personal, and when the imposition of punishment on a status or on conduct can only be justified by reference to the relationship of that status or conduct to other concededly criminal activity . . . that relationship must be sufficiently substantial to satisfy the concept of personal guilt in order to withstand attack under the Due Process Clause of the Fifth Amendment.[22]

The Court explained that groups often engage in both lawful and unlawful activities and that both the Due Process Clause and the First Amendment forbid punishing individuals who support only a group's lawful ends.[23] Driven by these constitutional concerns, the Court interpreted the Smith Act to require proof that an individual specifically intended to further the unlawful ends of the Communist Party. The Court then extended that principle in subsequent cases to bar imposition even of civil penalties—including tort liability[24] and denial of employment,[25] security clearance,[26] passports,[27] and even access to student meeting rooms[28]—absent proof of specific intent to further a group's unlawful activity.

These constitutional bulwarks, however, have not ended the desire for preventive law enforcement in times of crisis. Government officials pressed by the public to prevent the next terrorist attack, but barred by history and the Constitution from targeting people for their speech or associations, have sought to develop other ways of implementing preventive law enforcement. The principal substantive innovation in the war on terrorism has been the targeting of material support to terrorist groups.

Material Support

The prohibition of material support to terrorist organizations is a key tactic in the government's current war on terrorism. Federal law makes it a deportable offense and a crime to provide "material support" to terrorist organizations,[29] and the United States has pushed other nations to enact similar laws.[30] Most of the criminal "terrorism" cases that the government has filed since September 11 have included a charge that the defendant provided material support to a terrorist organization.[31] The government has closed down three of the largest Muslim charities in the United States based on broad allegations of potential terrorist financing.[32]

The reason the material support laws have proven so popular with federal prosecutors is that, like the speech and membership provisions of World War I and the Cold War, these laws do not require proof that an individual engaged in, or even intended to further, any terrorist activity. Under the criminal material support statute, for example, it is a crime to provide material support—defined expansively to include any "physical asset," as well as "personnel," "training," or "expert advice or assistance"[33]—to a designated terrorist organization, without regard to the purpose or effect of the actual support provided.[34] Under this law it would be a crime for a Quaker to send a book on Gandhi's theory of nonviolence—a "physical asset"—to the leader of a terrorist organization in hopes of persuading him to forgo violence. Indeed, the Quaker would have no defense even if he could show that his efforts had succeeded in convincing the group to end its violent ways. Similarly, if this law had been on the books in the 1980s, the thousands of Americans who donated money to the African National Congress (ANC) for its lawful political struggle against apartheid would face lengthy prison terms, because during those years the ANC was designated as a terrorist organization by the U.S. State Department.

The material support law is a classic instance of guilt by association. It imposes liability regardless of an individual's own intentions or purposes, based solely on the individual's connection to others who have committed illegal acts. Moreover, it imposes liability highly selectively. The law does not prohibit all material support to foreign organizations or even all material support to foreign organizations that use violence. Rather, it selectively prohibits material support only to those groups that the secretary of state chooses to designate. The statute gives the secretary of state a virtual blank check in designating groups; he can designate any foreign organization that has ever used or threatened to use a weapon against person or property and whose activities are contrary to our foreign policy, national defense, or economic interests.[35] Undoubtedly thousands of groups around the world meet the first criterion, and therefore, the second criterion does virtually all the work in selecting the handful that actually get designated.[36] Yet, because the secretary of state defines our foreign policy, his determination that a group's activities undermine our foreign policy is unreviewable.[37]

The government contends that the material support statute does not violate the Supreme Court's guilt by association principle because it does not criminalize membership per se, but only material support. The government argues that people remain free to join or associate with designated "foreign terrorist organizations" and are barred merely from providing them any material support. On this view, adopted thus far by the Court of Appeals for the Ninth Circuit, the prohibition on guilt by association applies only to laws that hinge penalties on membership alone.[38]

But the distinction between association and material support is illusory. Groups cannot exist without the material support of their members and associates. If the right of association meant only that one had the right to join organizations but not to support them, the right would be empty. Indeed, if this view were correct, all the laws that the Supreme Court faulted for imposing guilt by association could have been cured simply by hinging penalties not on the fact of membership, but on dues payments, volunteering, or monetary contributions—the very evidence generally advanced to prove membership. When the Supreme Court insisted so strongly on the prohibition on guilt by association, surely it did not mean for it to be vulnerable to such a formalistic end run.

It is precisely for this reason that the Court has consistently treated soliciting donations and making contributions as acts of association protected by the First Amendment. As the Supreme Court has said, "The right to join together 'for the advancement of beliefs and ideas' . . . is diluted if it does not include the right to pool money through contributions, for funds are often essential if 'advocacy' is to be truly or optimally 'effective.'"[39] The Court has permitted the capping of political campaign contributions, but only after concluding that the limits were imposed neutrally across the board and satisfied heightened scrutiny.[40] The material support law, by contrast, is analogous to a law permitting the Federal Election Commission to selectively criminalize all donations to any political party that it determines engages in some illegal activity and undermines American policy.

Some argue that the guilt by association principle ought not apply to the provision of material support to terrorist groups because money is fungible, so any support of a terrorist group will at a minimum have the indirect effect of furthering terrorism.[41] In enacting the criminal material support statute, for example, Congress found that "foreign organizations that engage in terrorist activity are so tainted by their criminal conduct that any contribution to such an organization facilitates that conduct."[42] But this is less a factual "finding" than a normative assertion. The legislative history of the material support law contains not one word of testimony about even a single terrorist organization's finances, much less all "foreign organizations that engage in terrorist activity." A congressional "finding" that "domestic political parties that engage in illegal conduct are so tainted by their criminal conduct that any contribution facilitates that conduct" surely would not authorize imposing guilt by association on support of domestic groups. It should have no greater effect with respect to "foreign terrorist organizations."

To be sure, money is fungible. But that is true of all money and all groups, domestic or foreign, political parties or militant terrorists. And for that reason, the argument proves far too much. If accepted, it would mean that legislatures could penalize material support of any organization that has ever engaged in any illegal activity, without regard to the purpose and use of any particular provision of material support. The state could make it a crime to provide newspapers or social services to gang members, to pay dues to the Communist Party, or to make a donation to the Republican Party, on the grounds that each of these organizations has engaged and may in the future engage in some illegal activity and that giving them material support would free up resources that could then be used to further the group's illegal ends. The United States unsuccessfully made just such a broad freeing-up argument to the Supreme Court in *Scales v. United States* as a reason for rejecting the specific intent test.[43] The argument should hold no greater sway today.

Finally, the freeing-up argument surely overstates the extent to which donations to a group's lawful activities are in practice translated into illegal activities. No one would seriously suggest, for example, that the millions of dollars donated to the ANC in the 1980s to support its lawful antiapartheid work were simply transformed into bombs and weapons for its military wing. Most "terrorist organizations" do not exist for the purpose of engaging in terrorism. They generally have a political purpose or goal—for example, ending apartheid in South Africa or obtaining self-determination for Palestinians in the occupied territories—and use a variety of means to attain that end. Some of those means may be terrorist, and some may be lawful. But there is no reason to believe that all organizations that use or threaten to use violence will turn any donation that supports their lawful activities into money for terrorism.

Cutting off material support for terrorist *activity* is undoubtedly a worthy and appropriate goal. But that can be done without indulging in guilt by association. When the Antiterrorism and Effective Death Penalty Act of 1996 added the current material support provision, it was already a crime to provide material support to anyone—individual, group, or government—for the purpose of engaging in terrorist activity.[44] Similarly, as the war on organized crime demonstrated, racketeering and money-laundering laws authorize the government to criminalize fronts used to support criminal activity and the laundering of money for illegal purposes. These laws permit the government to punish those who raise funds for terrorist activity without penalizing constitutionally protected associational activity.[45] The government recently obtained a guilty plea from the director of a Chicago-based Muslim charity on charges of racketeering in connection with diverting charitable contributions to support rebels in Chechnya.[46] The government's rhetorical case against the director was based on guilt by association—it charged, for example, that he was associated with al Qaeda leaders, failing to acknowledge that his alleged associations occurred in the 1980s, when the United States itself was supporting future al Qaeda leaders in their fight against the Soviet-backed government of Afghanistan. But rhetoric aside, the government's legal charges did not rest on guilt by association.

An organization like al Qaeda may present a special case, for it does not appear to have legal purposes at all. Unlike, say, the Irish Republican Army, the Palestinian Liberation Organization, or the ANC, groups with political agendas that use violent means among many others, al Qaeda appears to do little more than plot, train for, and conduct terrorism. But if that is the case, we do not need guilt by association to convict its supporters. It ought to be relatively simple to establish that when an individual affirmatively supports al Qaeda, he intends to support its terrorist ends, because al Qaeda has few if any other ends.

The extent to which the material support statute imposes guilt by association is illustrated by two current cases. In the first, the Humanitarian Law Project (HLP) has challenged the constitutionality of the material support statute as it applies to the HLP's conduct.[47] The HLP, a long-standing human rights organization based in Los Angeles, provided training and other assistance to the Kurdistan Workers' Party (PKK) in Turkey before the material support statute was passed. In particular, the HLP trained the PKK in human rights advocacy and peace negotiation skills, seeking to support a much-abused Kurdish minority in Turkey, while encouraging peaceful resolution of the conflict between the Kurds and the Turkish government. Once the material support statute was passed and the secretary of state designated the PKK a "terrorist organization," the HLP and its members would have faced lengthy prison terms had they continued to provide this training.

In the second case, federal prosecutors charged six young men from Lackawanna, New York, with providing material support to al Qaeda by attending one of its Afghanistan training camps.[48] To the government, the six were part of a "sleeper cell," ready and willing to engage in terrorism as soon as the call came. To the defense, they were a group of misguided religious idealists who found themselves in the training camp but returned from the trip never intending to engage in violent action of any kind. The remarkable thing is that under the statute's expansive reach, the government wins whichever version is true, because it need not prove that the individuals actually intended to undertake or even to further any terrorist act whatsoever. All six ultimately pleaded guilty, reportedly driven in part by concerns that they might otherwise be classified as "enemy combatants" and held incommunicado in military custody.[49]

Like the sedition laws of World War I and the communist membership provisions of the Cold War, the material support law allows the government to imprison individuals without proving that they ever sought to further a single act of terrorism. This makes preventive law enforcement much easier, because it gives the government discretion to go after "suspicious" individuals even where it lacks sufficient evidence to charge them with actually perpetrating, planning, or supporting a terrorist crime. But as the Cold War so vividly demonstrated, the statute's breadth makes it virtually inevitable that the government will target and penalize many innocent persons and deter a great deal of nonviolent associational activity.

II. THE COURSE OF LEAST RESISTANCE—SUBSTITUTING ADMINISTRATIVE PROCESS FOR CRIMINAL JUSTICE

Expanding the substantive scope of criminal prohibitions is only the most obvious way to achieve preventive law enforcement. Far more insidious, and far more common, is the exploitation of administrative procedures to avoid the rigors of the criminal process altogether. Administrative processes have proven highly effective in chilling officially disfavored activity in large part because they can be applied without affording their targets the rights of a criminal defendant. But because the rights that attach to the criminal process are for the most part intended to ensure that we do not imprison innocent people, resort to administrative processes that lack these protections carries with it the potential for widespread abuse.

Enemy Aliens

Perhaps the paradigmatic example of an administrative mechanism for preventive law enforcement is the Enemy Alien Act of 1798.[50] This law—enacted along with the Alien and Sedition Acts but, unlike them, still with us more than two hundred years later—authorizes the president during a declared war to lock up, deport, or otherwise restrict the liberty of any person over fourteen years of age who is a citizen of the country with which we are at war. It requires no individualized finding of culpability, dangerousness, or even suspicion. Because the law provides for deportation and detention without any process at all, it gives the government substantial power to engage in preventive detention. Detainees need not be provided hearings or lawyers, and the government need not prove anything beyond the fact of enemy citizenship. It represents the ultimate form of administrative control over potential threats.

Presidents invoked the Enemy Alien Act during the War of 1812,

World War I, and World War II to regulate the activities of all "enemy aliens" and to detain and deport some of them.[51] Since the law requires a formally declared war, it has not been used since World War II. The dangers of such authority were dramatically illustrated in World War II, when the government extended the rationale for detaining "enemy aliens" to intern some 110,000 persons—70,000 of whom were U.S. citizens—solely for their Japanese descent, without any individualized hearings or trials.[52] We have since formally apologized for that action and paid reparations to survivors. But the temptation to use administrative processes for preventive detention continues.

Immigration Processes—The Palmer Raids

In times of crisis that do not reach the level of a formally declared war, the government has relied on another form of administrative detention, also targeted at foreign nationals, using immigration law. The most infamous use of immigration authority for preventive detention purposes was in the Palmer Raids of the winter of 1919–20.[53] The raids were sparked by a series of terrorist bombings in the United States, including mail bombs addressed to Supreme Court Justice Oliver Wendell Holmes Jr. and numerous other government officials, and a bomb that destroyed part of Attorney General A. Mitchell Palmer's private home in Washington, DC. The government responded by mounting a mass nationwide roundup of foreign nationals, not for their role in the bombings but for their political associations with the Communist Party, the Communist Labor Party, and the Union of Russian Workers. The raids focused on foreign nationals because, lacking a peacetime sedition law, the immigration laws were the only authorization for targeting individuals for their politics. As Acting Secretary of Labor Louis Post observed, "The force of the delirium turned in the direction of a deportations crusade with the spontaneity of water flowing along the course of least resistance."[54]

The government ultimately arrested somewhere between four thousand and ten thousand individuals, many without any warrant, conducted illegal searches and seizures in doing so, detained many in overcrowded and unsanitary conditions, and interrogated them without lawyers.[55] The last tactic was seen as critical to obtaining the admissions of political association that would then form the basis for deportation. It was made possible by a last-minute rule change, enacted one business day before most of the arrests took place, that delayed the detainee's right to a lawyer (and to confrontation of the evidence upon which the arrest was based) until the case had "proceeded sufficiently in the development of the facts to protect the Government's interests."[56] Ultimately, more than five hundred foreign nationals were deported for their political associations; no one was charged with the bombings.[57] Louis Post, who oversaw most of the deportations and courageously cancelled several thousand deportations, later noted, "In no instance was it shown that the offending aliens had been connected in any way with bomb-throwing or bomb-placing or bomb-making. No explosives were found, nor any firearms except four pistols personally owned and some guns in the 'property room' of an amateur theatrical group."[58] Nonetheless, there was a limit to what Post could do; as he complained, the laws forced him "to order deportations of many aliens whom not even a lynching mob with the least remnant of righteous spirit would have deported from a frontier town."[59]

The government prefers immigration proceedings to criminal proceedings for many reasons. The Supreme Court has long ruled that deportation is not punishment and that, therefore, the rights attaching to criminal trials do not automatically extend to deportation hearings.[60] Foreign nationals in deportation proceedings have no constitutional right to a lawyer and have a statutory right to a lawyer only if they can find and afford one.[61] They have no constitutional right to a presumption of innocence beyond a reasonable doubt, to a jury trial, or to witness confrontation. The rules of evidence do not apply. The government asserts the right not only to rely on hearsay but also to deport, detain, and deny immigration benefits to noncitizens on the basis of secret evidence presented in camera and ex parte to the judge, so that neither the noncitizen nor his attorney has any right to confront or rebut it.[62] The Supreme Court has insisted that foreign nationals living in the United States have a due process right to a fundamentally fair hearing, but the contours of that right have not been clearly articulated.[63]

Emergency Administrative Detention

Given the judgment of history on the Japanese American internment of World War II, one might think that the very concept of extending administrative detention to citizens would have been quickly abandoned. Not so. In 1948, in the immediate aftermath of the war, the Justice Department secretly adopted a program, known as "the Portfolio," for interning "dangerous persons" during an emergency declared by the president.[64] Under this program, which applied to citizens and foreigners alike, the president would suspend the writ of habeas corpus, and mass arrests would be made under a single "master warrant" issued by the attorney general. The single warrant would also authorize widespread searches and seizures. Those detained would have no right to seek judicial review but would be limited to an administrative hearing before specially constituted boards of review not bound by the rules of evidence. Their only appeal would be to the president.[65]

In September 1950, Congress independently created its own detention plan, enacted as Title II of the Internal Security Act.[66] This statute, which remained on the books until 1971, also authorized emergency detention of dangerous persons, albeit under slightly more restrictive terms than "the Portfolio" provided. As Richard Longaker described Congress's detention program:

> [It authorized] detention without arraignment before a judge, the possibility of bail, or a jury trial. . . . Apprehension and incarceration were based on an administrative finding of prospective guilt in which non-judicial officers utilized a standard of reasonable belief, not probable cause, that a suspect should be held. . . . The authority of the Attorney General was uncontrolled. He could issue warrants at will and withhold evidence selectively, including the identity of the detainee's accusers, thus bypassing the right of a defendant to confront and cross-examine his accusers.[67]

In 1952, Congress authorized and funded detention centers for suspected subversives in Arizona, California, Florida, Oklahoma, and Pennsylvania.[68]

No one was ever detained under these programs because no emergency arose. But the very fact that for more than a generation after World War II the federal government planned to detain "dangerous" citizens and foreigners wholly outside the criminal process illustrates how far the notion of substituting administrative process for criminal justice had spread. In addition, the mere existence of these authorities justified the FBI in undertaking widespread political spying for decades so that it could maintain lists of suspicious persons to be detained in a future emergency. At its peak in 1954, the FBI's "Security

Index" of people to be detained numbered 26,174 persons.[69] In the 1960s, the FBI's list included civil rights and antiwar movement activists, including Dr. Martin Luther King Jr.[70] In the late 1960s, the FBI instructed its agents to investigate for potential inclusion on the lists the Students for a Democratic Society, other "pro-Communist New Left-type groups," and even all persons living in "communes."[71]

It was not until 1971 that Congress repealed the emergency detention provisions and enacted a provision stating that "no citizen shall be imprisoned or otherwise detained by the United States except pursuant to an Act of Congress."[72] Yet the FBI continued to maintain lists of subversive persons until at least 1975, when it revealed the existence of the lists to a congressional committee investigating intelligence abuses and abolished the lists.[73]

Loyalty Review Boards and Congressional Committee Hearings

During the Cold War, as noted earlier, the government expressly made subversive speech and association a crime under the Smith Act. The vast majority of those harmed by the excesses of the Cold War, however, were targeted not through the criminal process but by loyalty review procedures and congressional committee hearings. In both settings, the government was able to inflict a kind of punishment while denying its targets critical criminal protections, such as the presumption of innocence and the right to confront the prosecution's evidence.

Loyalty review processes were applied to every federal employee, as well as to many nonfederal employees, through copycat programs implemented by state and local governments and by private employers seeking to do business with the government. The ostensible targets were disloyal employees. But disloyal was for all practical purposes reduced to "Communist," and one could lose one's job not only for membership in the Party, but even for "sympathetic association" with suspected Communists.[74] As in the immigration setting, the government successfully argued that it need not provide the rights that would apply in a criminal process because denying someone a job did not constitute punishment. Indeed, the courts generally went even further, holding that because employees did not have a liberty or property interest in retaining their jobs, they were not even entitled to due process.[75]

Consider, for example, the case of Dorothy Bailey.[76] In 1949, Bailey, a personnel trainer with the Civil Service Commission in Washington, DC, lost her job. A loyalty review board had found that there were "reasonable grounds" to suspect that she was disloyal to the United States. Ms. Bailey never learned the source of those grounds. She was told only in the most general terms that she was suspected of having been associated with the Communist Party, the American League for Peace and Democracy, and the Washington Committee for Democratic Action, all organizations designated by the attorney general as suspect. At her hearing, she was represented by three of the nation's leading lawyers—Thurman Arnold, Abe Fortas, and Paul Porter—and she put on a vigorous defense. She admitted past membership in the American League but denied all other charges. She asserted her loyalty, offered seventy supporting affidavits and four witnesses to attest to her character, and submitted to all questioning by the hearing examiners. No witness offered evidence against her. As the Court of Appeals for the DC Circuit later summarized it, "The record consists entirely of evidence in her favor."[77] Yet the hearing board ruled against her on the basis of undisclosed secret FBI reports relaying accusations by unidentified informants. The court of appeals found nothing illegal or unconstitutional about the process, reasoning that since she had no right to a government job, she was entitled to no due process in her termination.[78] The Supreme Court affirmed the decision by an equally divided vote. In the end, the best Arnold, Fortas, and Porter could do for Bailey was to hire her as their office manager.[79]

Dorothy Bailey did not stand alone. Professor Brown estimated that because loyalty review programs were adopted by federal, state, and local governments and often extended to private employers who sought to do business with the government as well, as many as one in five working Americans was subjected to the loyalty review process in one way or another—by having to take an oath, filling out loyalty disclosure forms, or being subjected to a full-scale loyalty review hearings.[80]

Congressional hearings provided yet another way to effect preventive law enforcement without having to provide the safeguards of the criminal process. HUAC subpoenaed thousands of witnesses to testify about alleged communist sympathizers and to name names.[81] It operated on the theory of guilt by association, which, as Alan Barth described it, went in two directions: "A group was contaminated by any 'subversive' individual who entered it. And, conversely, every member of the group became 'subversive' by the mere fact of membership."[82] Because a congressional hearing is not a criminal trial and does not take any liberty or property interest from the witness, HUAC maintained that it did not need to provide witnesses with even the rights associated with a civil trial. Witnesses were frequently confronted with accusations from unidentified informants and denied any opportunity to confront their accusers or to present their own witnesses. Yet the exposure of such proceedings often led private employers to fire those who appeared or were named there, and, therefore, HUAC's chilling effect was substantial.[83]

Alan Barth nicely summed up the use of congressional committees and administrative tribunals for political control during the Cold War.

> By the simple stratagem of charging a man with disloyalty, instead of with treason or espionage or sabotage, it is possible to evade the constitutional requirements that he be indicted by a grand jury, that he enjoy a speedy and public trial by an impartial petit jury, that he be informed of the nature and cause of the accusation and confronted with the witnesses against him, that he be accorded the benefit of compulsory process to obtain witnesses in his favor. He is indicted and tried and sentenced by congressional committee or administrative tribunal, with the same men acting as prosecutors, judges, and jury. The presumption of innocence supposed to surround him is ignored. The mere charge of disloyalty is treated as evidence of guilt.[84]

Administrative Process in the War on Terrorism

All of these measures are now seen as having spawned grave and widespread civil liberties abuses. The Palmer Raids were condemned contemporaneously by a blue-ribbon panel of lawyers, including the dean of the Harvard Law School and Professor Felix Frankfurter,[85] and history has confirmed their judgment. History has also decried the Japanese American internment, HUAC, and the loyalty review boards. These events have taught us that when the government is allowed to avoid the safeguards designed to protect the innocent, many innocents suffer. Yet today, our government has once again invoked similar administrative shortcuts in its pursuit of preventive justice.

Perhaps the most dramatic instance of the resort to administrative process in today's war on terrorism is the indefinite and virtually incommunicado detention of foreign nationals and U.S. citizens alike as "enemy combatants."[86] The Enemy Alien Act does not apply by its terms to the war on terrorism because we have not declared war on any nation; there are no citizens of al Qaeda. But the government has nonetheless sought to invoke military authority to bypass the criminal process, asserting unreviewable authority to detain in military custody any person whom the president labels an "enemy combatant." Under this authority, the government maintained that it could detain foreign nationals and U.S. citizens alike indefinitely, without a hearing, without access to a lawyer, and without judicial review, simply on the president's say-so. It has used that authority to hold more than 650 foreign nationals at a military base on Guantánamo Bay, Cuba,[87] and to hold two U.S. citizens—Yaser Hamdi and Jose Padilla—and a foreign national—Ali al-Marri—in naval brigs here in the United States.

With one exception, the lower courts ruled that the Guantánamo detainees have no right to judicial review of their detention because they are foreign nationals detained outside the jurisdiction of the United States.[88] With respect to the two U.S. citizens, the lower courts were less dismissive. Even the U.S. Court of Appeals for the Fourth Circuit, the most conservative federal court of appeals in the nation, rejected the government's "sweeping proposition" that the courts have no right to review the president's determination that a U.S. citizen is an "enemy combatant."[89] The government argued that if any judicial review of the president's "enemy combatant" designation were appropriate, at most the courts could ask only whether the president had "some evidence" to support the designation, and should conduct that inquiry without even hearing from the detainee, nor permit any confrontation or testing of the government's evidence.[90] In June 2004, the Supreme Court resoundingly rejected the government's position, ruling that foreign nationals on Guantánamo and U.S. citizens held here could challege the legality of their detention in federal courts, and that they were entitled to a hearing before a neutral adjudicator on whether they were in fact "enemy combatants."[91]

In addition to the "enemy combatant" designations, the government revived the Palmer Raids tactics, using its immigration authority to arrest and detain large numbers of persons without any showing that they were connected to terrorism. Shortly after September 11, Attorney General John Ashcroft announced that he would use every law on the books, including immigration law, to target and detain "suspected terrorists" in order to prevent future acts of terrorism.[92] Pursuant to that plan, the Justice Department reported that 1,182 individuals had been detained in the first seven weeks of the post–September 11 investigation.[93] After November 5, facing criticism that it had charged none of these "suspects" with any terrorist crimes, the Justice Department simply stopped issuing a running tally of its detentions.[94] But based solely on government figures, it is clear that over five thousand foreign nationals have been subject to antiterrorism preventive detention as of May 2004, two and a half years after the campaign began.[95]

The bulk of the detainees were held on immigration charges.[96] Many immigration detainees were held and tried in secret. Pursuant to directions from the attorney general, even where cases involved no classified information of any sort, the "special interest" 9/11 detention cases could not be listed on the public docket, no one could attend their hearings other than their lawyer, and the presiding judges could neither confirm nor deny that the cases even existed.[97] Many detainees were held initially without any charges at all for weeks.[98] Many found it difficult to find a lawyer, in part because the government radically restricted their ability to contact anyone outside the prison.[99] Many were held for months even after agreeing to depart the country, simply because the FBI had not yet completed its investigation of them.[100] All of this was possible only because the immigration process is administrative in nature. Were these individuals tried criminally, they would have had a right to a public trial, to be brought before an independent judge within forty-eight hours of their arrest, and not to be detained simply because the FBI had not completed its investigation.

Just as the Palmer Raids turned up no actual bombers and the McCarthy era tactics identified few spies or saboteurs, so too the government's yield of actual terrorists from its post-9/11 preventive detention program has been staggeringly small. According to Ashcroft, all of the detainees were "suspected terrorists." Yet of the approximately five thousand foreign nationals detained, only four have been charged with any crime relating to terrorism.[101] Two were acquitted on the terrorist charges at trial, and the conviction of a third is under a cloud because the prosecution failed to disclose to the defense evidence that its principal witness lied on the stand.[102] The fourth man awaits trial on charges that he conspired to set off a bomb in an Ohio shopping center in 2000. None of the detainees has been charged with involvement in the September 11 crimes, and the vast majority have been affirmatively cleared of any criminal charges by the FBI. The government's policy was to release and/or deport detainees only after the FBI had cleared them. Yet as of October 2002, Attorney General Ashcroft announced that the INS had deported 431 detainees, and in July 2002, the Justice Department reported that only 81 individuals remained in immigration detention.[103] Thus, by the government's own account, virtually none of those detained as "suspected terrorists" turned out to be terrorists.

A third administrative mechanism for "preventive" law enforcement is the International Emergency Economic Powers Act (IEEPA).[104] This law, designed to authorize the president to impose economic sanctions on foreign countries in emergency situations, has in recent years been adapted to the task of cutting off funds for designated "terrorist" groups and individuals. President Clinton first extended IEEPA to political organizations in 1995, when he declared a national emergency with respect to the Middle East peace process and designated twelve organizations—ten Palestinian organizations opposed to the peace process and two Jewish extremist groups—as "specially designated terrorists."[105] The Executive Order also permits the secretary of state to name additional specially designated terrorists if they are found to be "owned or controlled by, or to act for or on behalf of" an entity designated by the president.[106] Shortly after the September 11 attacks, President Bush issued an Executive Order imposing similar financial restrictions on "specially designated global terrorists," and also authorizing the secretary of treasury to add to the list anyone who "assist[s] in, sponsor[s], or provide[s] . . . support for" or is "otherwise associated" with a designated terrorist.[107] Designation results in the immediate blocking of all of the entity's assets and makes it a crime to engage in any economic transactions with the designated entity. The statute specifies no definition for identifying the entities initially designated by the president, leaving that critical decision entirely to the president's discretion. IEEPA affords those designated by the president no opportunity to contest the designation. Further, those groups and individuals subsequently identified by the secretary of treasury need only be found to be in some way "associated" with the initially designated entities.

IEEPA allows the president to selectively blacklist disfavored political groups without substantive standards or procedural safeguards, and now allows the secretary of treasury to extend those sanctions to individuals based solely on "associations," without regard to the character of the associations. In short, it resurrects the Cold War practice of generating official lists of proscribed organizations without clear substantive guidelines or meaningful procedural safeguards.

Moreover, a little-noticed provision in the USA Patriot Act, enacted in October 2001, amended the IEEPA to authorize the Treasury Department to freeze all assets of any organization merely on the assertion that it is under investigation for potentially violating the IEEPA. The amendment further authorizes the government to defend that freeze order if challenged in court with secret evidence, presented to the court in camera and ex parte.[108] Under the investigative provision, the Treasury Department after September 11 froze the assets of two Muslim charities, Global Relief Foundation, Inc., and Benevolence International Foundation. In both cases, it did so without a hearing or any specific charges; the groups were told only that they were "under investigation." And in both cases, the government searched the organizations' offices and seized all of their records, books, and computers. Both organizations, along with a third charity, the Holy Land Foundation, have now been listed as specially designated terrorists and specially designated global terrorists, based not on allegations of criminal conduct but on their alleged associations with other groups designated by the president.

Global Relief Foundation and the Holy Land Foundation challenged the freezing of their assets on multiple constitutional grounds, but the courts summarily dismissed the challenges, in part based on secret information submitted ex parte and in camera to the court and not provided to the foundations or their lawyers.[109] None of these foundations has been charged with any criminal conduct of any kind, yet all three have been put out of business through these administrative measures.

The lengths to which IEEPA sanctions can be extended are best illustrated by the case of Mohammed Salah, the first American citizen to be listed as a specially designated terrorist. Salah was arrested, interrogated, and convicted in Israel, allegedly on the basis of a coerced confession, for having distributed money to the families of deported leaders of Hamas in the 1990s. He served a five-year sentence in an Israeli jail, was freed, and returned to the United States.[110] In 1995, however, he was listed as a specially designated terrorist.[111] He had no opportunity to present evidence concerning the circumstances of his confession, his activities in Israel, or anything else. He had no trial, no notice, and no appeal. And as a specially designated terrorist, it became a crime for anyone in the United States to have any economic transactions whatsoever with him. Literally applied, the designation would bar him from buying a loaf of bread from the corner grocer, going to a doctor, hiring a lawyer, or even taking a donation from a friend. In short, he has been subjected to a sort of internal banishment, which, if literally enforced, would lead to his starvation without so much as a hearing, much less a trial.[112]

Military custody, immigration detention, and administrative embargoes have all permitted the government to exercise control over "suspicious" individuals and groups without having to prove that any criminal activity was performed, planned, or even contemplated. But precisely because these legal mechanisms—which can have quite devastating effects on their targets—do not require any individualized proof of wrongdoing, they have been and inevitably will be misused against persons engaged in no terrorist or other criminal activity at all.

CONCLUSION

Those who claim that the United States has avoided the mistakes of the past in its current war on terrorism have failed to look beneath the surface. While it is true that the scope of the wrongs done during World War I, World War II, or the Cold War has not yet been equaled, we are only in the initial stages of a war likely to be as permanent as the war on drugs or the war on crime. And when one looks not at the quantity but at the quality of our response, it is clear that we have resurrected many of the very techniques that got us into trouble in the past—namely, expanding the substantive definitions of wrongdoing to encompass otherwise innocent political activity, relying on group identity rather than individual conduct for suspicion, and adopting administrative measures to avoid the safeguards associated with the criminal process.

If the past is any guide, these mistakes will come at substantial cost to the targeted communities, as many innocent persons are swept up in the government's preventive net. But the mistakes may also undermine the war on terrorism itself. Professor Oren Gross has argued that the greatest threat that terrorists pose to a democratic state is not to its physical survival, but to what one might call the survival of principle.[113] He argues that what terrorists want is to provoke the state into overreacting in ways that violate its own principles, thereby undermining the state's legitimacy and creating sympathy for those allied with the terrorists.[114] If that is the case, it is all the more critical that we learn from our past mistakes and adhere to the principles that distinguish us from terrorists, for we may well be playing into al Qaeda's hands.

Nearly three years after the United States suffered one of the worst attacks on civilian life in modern history, one might expect to find widespread sympathy and support for the United States around the world. But instead, reports of anti-Americanism suggest that hostility to the United States has grown substantially since September 11, and has never been higher.[115] No doubt much of this resentment is attributable to our unilateral foreign policy. But it likely is also due at least in part to the fact that as we insist that we are fighting a war for our freedom, we have denied those basic freedoms to many "suspicious" persons, the vast majority of whom are foreign nationals of Arab origin and/or Muslim faith. When we sacrifice the very principles that distinguish us from terrorists, and particularly when we do so in ways that appear to discriminate, we forfeit much of the legitimacy of the effort to protect ourselves from terrorism.

It is understandable that in times of fear, we defer to authority and close our eyes to the wrongs perpetrated in the name of our protection. But history reveals that blind faith is wholly unwarranted. Now more than ever it is critical that we remain true to our principles. There is nothing wrong with prevention when it consists of protecting potential targets of attack or stepping up security at borders, airports, and other vulnerable points. But when prevention translates into the punishment of individuals for what we suspect they may do, rather than for what they have done, it cannot be justified in a democratic society. The safeguards of the criminal process exist for a reason, and whenever we impose punishment or deprive persons of their liberty without adhering to these safeguards, we are likely to do more harm than good. The success of the war on terrorism, and indeed of our democratic experiment, requires us to reconsider the shortcuts that we have all too swiftly and predictably adopted.

NOTES

I am or was counsel in several of the cases discussed herein, including *Reno v. American-Arab Anti-Discrimination Committee,* 525 U.S. 471 (1999); *Turkmen v. Ashcroft,* No. CV-02–307 (E.D.N.Y. 2002); *Humanitarian Law Project v. Reno,* 205 F.3d 1130 (9th Cir. 2000), *cert. denied,* 532 U.S. 904 (2001). Kate Didech provided excellent research assistance. This article initially appeared in a slightly modified form in 38 *Harvard Civil Rights—Civil Liberties Law Review* 1 (2003).

1. Ralph S. Brown Jr., *Loyalty and Security: Employment Tests in the United States* (New Haven: Yale University Press, 1958), 14.

2. See, e.g., Jack Goldsmith and Cass R. Sunstein, "Military Tribunals and Legal Culture: What a Difference Sixty Years Makes," *Constitutional Commentary* 19 (2002): 261; Eric Muller, "War, Liberty, and the Lessons of History," *West Virginia Law Review* 104 (2002): 571; Pam Belluck, "Hue and Murmur over Curbed Rights," *New York Times,* Nov. 17, 2001, B8; Marty Meehan, Editorial, "More Tools Needed to Fight Terrorism," *Boston Herald,* Oct. 3, 2001, at 29; Jeffrey Rosen, "Liberty Wins: So Far; Bush Runs into Checks and Balances in Demanding New Powers," *Washington Post,* Sept. 15, 2002, B2; Jeffrey Rosen, "What Price Security? Testing the Resilience of American Values," *New York Times,* Nov. 18, 2001, § 4, 1.

3. Brown, *supra* note 1.

4. See Am. Immigration Lawyers Ass'n, *Immigration, Security, and Civil Liberties* (AILA Issue Paper No. 21ip2001, May 30, 2002), available at http://www.aila.org/contentViewer.aspx?bc=9,722,808; Neil A. Lewis and Christopher Marquis, "Longer Visa Waits for Arabs; Stir over U.S. Eavesdropping," *New York Times,* Nov. 10, 2001, A1; Susan Sachs, "For Many American Muslims, Complaints of Quiet but Persistent Bias," *New York Times,* Apr. 25, 2002, A16; Susan Sachs, "Government Ready to Fingerprint and Keep Track of Some Foreign Visitors," *New York Times,* Sept. 9, 2002, A16.

5. See Jonathan Schell, *The Fate of the Earth* (New York: Alfred A. Knopf, 1982) (on the threat of nuclear annihilation).

6. John Lord O'Brian, *National Security and Individual Freedom* (Cambridge: Harvard University Press, 1955), 24–25.

7. *United States v. Rahman,* 189 F.3d 88 (2d Cir. 1999), *cert. denied,* 528 U.S. 1094 (2000).

8. Sedition Act of 1918, ch. 75, 40 Stat. 553, *repealed by* Act of Mar. 3, 1921, ch. 136, 41 Stat. 1359.

9. See Zechariah Chafee, *Free Speech in the United States* (Cambridge: Harvard University Press, 1948), 51.

10. *Gilbert v. Minnesota,* 254 U.S. 325 (1920); *Abrams v. United States,* 250 U.S. 616 (1919); *Debs v. United States,* 249 U.S. 211 (1919); *Frohwerk v. United States,* 249 U.S. 204 (1919); *Schenck v. United States,* 249 U.S. 47 (1919).

11. See Peter H. Irons, "Fighting Fair: Zechariah Chafee, Jr., The Department of Justice, and the Trial at the Harvard Club," *Harvard Law Review* 94 (1981): 1205.

12. Stephen Buckley, "The Al-Arian Argument," *St. Petersburg Times,* Mar. 3, 2002, 1A, 2002 WL 15926430; Sharon Walsh, "Blaming the Victim? A University Vows to Fire a Tenured Professor Facing Death Threats in the Wake of September 11," *Chronicle of Higher Education,* Feb. 8, 2002, A10.

13. "Report of Academic Freedom and Tenure Investigation of University of South Florida," *Academe,* May/June 2003, available at http://www.aaup.org/Com-a/institutions/usf.htm; Press Release, American Association of University Professors, "An Interim Statement on Al-Arian," released June 8, 2002, available at http://www.aaup.org/newsroom/press/2002/02–6usf .htm (stating that "the investigating committee believes that Professor Al-Arian's statements fell well within the ambit of academic freedom" and that "other currently pending charges against Professor Al-Arian have been characterized by the investigating committee as too insubstantial to warrant serious consideration as adequate cause for dismissal"); see also Rob Brannon, "AAUP Restates Stern Warning to USF," *University of South Florida Oracle,* June 13, 2002, available at http://www.usforacle.com/vnews/display.v/ART/2002/06/13/3d088a6e2c734?in_archive=1.

14. Hugh Gusterson, "The Weakest Link? Academic Dissent in the 'War on Terrorism'" (this vol.). The revised and expanded ACTA report, released in February 2002, is available at http://www.goacta.org/Reports/defciv.pdf. The originally issued version of the report included the names and statements of individual professors, but after considerable negative media coverage, the organization issued an edited version without naming individuals. The original report, issued in November 2001, is available at http://www.eecs.harvard.edu/~aaron/defciv.pdf. See generally Emily Eakin, "On the Lookout for Patriotic Incorrectness," *New York Times,* Nov. 24, 2001, A15.

15. In testimony before the Senate Judiciary Committee, Attorney General Ashcroft stated: "To those who pit Americans against immigrants and citizens against non-citizens; to those who scare peace-loving people with phantoms of lost liberty; my message is this: Your tactics only aid terrorists—for they erode our national unity and diminish our resolve. They give ammunition to America's enemies, and pause to America's friends." *DOJ Oversight: Preserving our Freedoms while Defending against Terrorism: Hearing before the Senate Comm. on the Judiciary,* 107th Cong. (2001), available at http://www.senate.gov/%7Ejudiciary/testimony.cfm?id=121&wit_id=42. Criticism of Ashcroft's statement was quick to follow. See, e.g., Dan Eggen, "Ashcroft Defends Anti-Terrorism Steps; Civil Liberties Groups' Attacks 'Only Aid Terrorists,' Senate Panel Told," *Washington Post,* Dec. 7, 2001, A1; Neil A. Lewis, "Ashcroft Defends Antiterror Plan; Says Criticism May Aid U.S. Foes," *New York Times,* Dec. 7, 2001, A1; Frank Rich, "Confessions of a Traitor," *New York Times,* Dec. 8, 2001, A23; Editorial, "John Ashcroft Misses the Point," *New York Times,* Dec. 7, 2001, A30; Editorial, "Shades of Gray," *St. Louis Post-Dispatch,* Dec. 9, 2001, B2; Editorial, "On Civil Liberties: Under Cloak of 'Security,'" *San Francisco Chronicle,* Dec. 9, 2001, D4, 2001 WL 3422016.

16. By its terms, the Smith Act punished speech—advocacy of the overthrow of the United States government by force or violence—and many Com-

munists, including the national leadership of the party, were prosecuted for conspiracy to so advocate and for conspiracy to organize a group to so advocate. See generally *United States v. Dennis,* 341 U.S. 494 (1951); Michael Belknap, *Cold War Political Justice: The Smith Act, the Communist Party, and American Civil Liberties* (Westport, CT: Greenwood Press, 1977); Arthur J. Sabin, *In Calmer Times: The Supreme Court and Red Monday* (Philadelphia: University of Pennsylvania Press, 1999); William M. Wiecek, "The Legal Foundations of Domestic Anticommunism: The Background of *Dennis v. United States,*" *Supreme Court Review 2001* (2001): 375.

17. Eleanor Bontecou, *The Federal Loyalty-Security Program* (Ithaca: Cornell University Press, 1953), 171; see id. at 157–204 (discussing the makeup, evolution, and uses of the attorney general's lists).

18. See *Yates v. United States,* 354 U.S. 298, 318 (1957). The *Yates* decision effectively ended prosecutions under the advocacy sections of the Smith Act. See Sabin, *supra* note 16.

19. 395 U.S. 444 (1969).

20. *NAACP v. Claiborne Hardware Co.,* 458 U.S. 886, 932 (1982) (citations omitted).

21. 7 U.S. 203 (1961).

22. *Id.* at 224–25.

23. *Id.* at 224–25, 229–30.

24. *NAACP v. Claiborne Hardware Co.,* 458 U.S. at 932.

25. See *Elfbrandt v. Russell,* 384 U.S. 11, 19 (1966).

26. See *United States v. Robel,* 389 U.S. 258, 265–66 (1967).

27. See *Aptheker v. Sec'y of State,* 378 U.S. 500, 510–12 (1964).

28. See *Healy v. James,* 408 U.S. 169, 186–87 (1972).

29. 8 U.S.C. § 1182(a)(3)(B)(iv)(VI) (West Supp. 2002); 18 U.S.C.A. § 2339B (West 2000 and Supp. 2002).

30. See, e.g., International Convention for the Suppression of the Financing of Terrorism, G.A. Res. 54/109, U.N. GAOR, 4th Sess., U.N. Doc. A/RES/54/109 (1999); Kurt Eichenwald, "Global Plan to Track Terror Funds," *New York Times,* Dec. 19, 2001, B5; Jeff Gerth and Judith Miller, "Report Says Saudis Fail to Crack Down on Charities That Finance Terrorists," *New York Times,* Oct. 17, 2002, A20; Serge Schmemann, "U.N. Gets a Litany of Antiterror Plans," *New York Times,* Jan. 12, 2002, A7.

31. John Walker Lindh, the so-called American Taliban, was charged with providing material support to two terrorist organizations by attending their training camps. See Indictment at 10–14, *United States v. Lindh,* No. CR. 02–37a (E.D. Va. Oct. 4, 2002), available at http://news.findlaw.com/hdocs/docs/terrorism/uswlindh020502cmp.html. Lynne Stewart, the attorney for Sheikh Omar Abdel Rahman, has been charged with providing material support to an Egyptian terrorist organization by facilitating communications between the Sheikh and the group. See Indictment at 10–20, *United States v. Sattar,* No. CR. 02–395 (S.D.N.Y. Apr. 4, 2002), available at http://news.findlaw.com/hdocs/docs/terrorism/ussattar040902ind.pdf. Five young men from Lackawanna, New York, have been charged under the material support statute for attending

an al Qaeda training camp. See Indictment, *United States v. Goba,* No. 02-M-107 (W.D.N.Y. Oct. 21, 2002), available at http://news.findlaw.com/hdocs/docs/terrorism/usgoba102102ind.html. James Ujaama, a Seattle activist, has been charged with providing material support by planning to set up a training camp in the United States for al Qaeda. See Indictment, *United States v. Ujaama* (W.D. Wash. Aug. 28, 2002), available at http://news.findlaw.com/hdocs/docs/ terrorism/usujaama82802ind.pdf. A group in Portland has been charged under the material support statute for seeking to fight in Afghanistan on behalf of al Qaeda. See Indictment at 12–13, *United States v. Battle,* CR-02–399 (D. Or. Oct. 3, 2002), available at http://news.findlaw.com/hdocs/docs/terrorism/usbattle100302ind.pdf. Finally, a group of men in Detroit has been charged under the same statute for allegedly operating as an underground support unit for terrorist attacks and a "sleeper" operational combat cell. See Indictment at 6–17, *United States v. Koubriti,* No. 01–80778 (E.D. Mich. Aug. 28, 2002), available at http://news.findlaw.com/hdocs/docs/terrorism/usk-oubriti82802ind.pdf.

32. See John Mintz, "Muslim Charity Leader Indicted," *Washington Post,* Oct. 10, 2002, A14 (Benevolence International Foundation); John Mintz, "U.S. Labels Muslim Charity as Terrorist Group," *Washington Post,* Oct. 19, 2002, A2 (Global Relief Foundation); John Mintz and Neely Tucker, "Judge Backs U.S. on Assets Seizure," *Washington Post,* Aug. 10, 2002, A12 (Holy Land Foundation for Relief and Development).

33. 18 U.S.C.A. § 2339A(b) (West Supp. 2002) (defining material support or resources as "currency or monetary instruments or financial securities, financial services, lodging, training, expert advice or assistance, safehouses, false documentation or identification, communications equipment, facilities, weapons, lethal substances, explosives, personnel, transportation, and other physical assets, except medicine or religious materials").

34. 18 U.S.C.A. § 2339B (West 2000 and Supp. 2002).

35. See 8 U.S.C.A § 1189(a)(1), (c)(2) (West 1999 and Supp. 2002) (setting forth criteria for designation of terrorist organizations).

36. The secretary of state's first designation under the law listed thirty organizations. Designation of Foreign Terrorist Organizations, 62 Fed. Reg. 52,650 (Oct. 8, 1997). The list has expanded since September 11, but still includes only thirty-five organizations. Fact Sheet, Office of Counterterrorism, U.S. Department of State, Foreign Terrorist Organizations (Oct. 23, 2002), available at http://www.state.gov/s/ct/rls/fs/2002/12389.htm. Prominent terrorist groups like the Irish Republican Army are notably not on the list.

37. *Peoples' Mojahedin Org. of Iran v. United States Dept of State,* 182 F.3d 17, 23 (D.C. Cir. 1999) (holding that the secretary of state's determination that an organization's activities undermine national foreign policy for purposes of designating terrorist groups is a judicially unreviewable political question), *cert. denied,* 529 U.S. 1104 (2000).

38. See *Humanitarian Law Project v. Reno,* 205 F.3d 1130, 1133 (9th Cir. 2000), *cert. denied,* 532 U.S. 904 (2001).

39. *Buckley v. Valeo,* 424 U.S. 1, 65–66 (1976) (quoting *NAACP v. Alabama ex*

rel. Patterson, 357 U.S. 449, 460 (1958)). Monetary contributions to political organizations are a protected form of association and expression. See id. at 16–17, 24–25; *Citizens against Rent Control/Coalition for Fair Housing v. City of Berkeley,* 454 U.S. 290, 295–96 (1981) (holding that monetary contributions to a group are a form of "collective expression" protected by the right of association); *In re* Asbestos Litig., 46 F.3d 1284, 1290 (3d Cir. 1994) (holding that contributions to political organizations are constitutionally protected absent specific intent to further a group's illegal ends); *Serv. Employees Int'l Union v. Fair Political Practices Comm'n,* 955 F.2d 1312, 1316 (9th Cir. 1992) (stating that "contributing money is an act of political association that is protected by the First Amendment").

40. See *Buckley,* 424 U.S. at 28.

41. See *Humanitarian Law Project,* 205 F.3d at 1134; Gerald Neuman, "Terrorism, Selective Deportation, and the First Amendment after *Reno v. AADC,*" *Georgetown Immigration Law Journal* 14 (2000): 313, 329–30.

42. Antiterrorism and Effective Death Penalty Act of 1996, Pub. L. No. 104–132, § 301(a)(7), 110 Stat. 1214, 1247.

43. Brief for the United States on Reargument at 8, *Scales v. United States,* 367 U.S. 203 (1961) (No. 1) (arguing that a showing of "specific intent" is unnecessary "on the principle that knowingly joining an organization with illegal objectives contributes to the attainment of those objectives because of the support given by membership itself").

44. See 18 U.S.C.A. § 2339A (West Supp. 2002) (criminalizing material support of terrorist activity).

45. See Racketeer Influenced and Corrupt Organizations (RICO) Act, 18 U.S.C.A. §§ 1961–1968 (West 2000 and Supp. 2002); Money Laundering Control Act of 1986, 18 U.S.C.A. §§ 1956–1957 (West 2000 and Supp. 2002) (forfeiture of property is authorized by 18 U.S.C.A. §§ 981–982 (West 2000 and Supp. 2002)).

46. See Indictment, *United States v. Arnaout,* No. 02-CR-892 (N.D. Ill. Nov. 1, 2002), available at http://news.findlaw.com/hdocs/docs/terrorism/usarnaout10902ind.pdf.

47. *Humanitarian Law Project v. Reno,* 205 F.3d 1130, 1133 (9th Cir. 2000), *cert. denied,* 532 U.S. 904 (2001).

48. See Indictment, *United States v. Goba,* No. 02-M-107 (W.D. New York Oct. 8, 2002), available at http://news.findlaw.com/hdocs/docs /terrorism/usgoba102102ind.html.

49. Dan Herbeck, "Lackawanna Six: Two Defendants Feel Pressure for Plea Deal," *Buffalo News,* April 6, 2003.

50. 50 U.S.C. §§ 21–24 (2000).

51. See generally J. Gregory Sidak, "War, Liberty, and Enemy Aliens," *New York University Law Review* 67 (1992): 1402.

52. See David Cole, "Enemy Aliens," *Stanford Law Review* 54 (2002): 953, 989–94.

53. See generally Robert K. Murray, *Red Scare: A Study in National Hysteria, 1919–1920* (New York: McGraw-Hill, 1955); Louis F. Post, *The Deportations Delirium of Nineteen-Twenty: A Personal Narrative of an Historic Official Experience*

(Chicago: C. H. Kerr, 1923); William Preston Jr., *Aliens and Dissenters: Federal Suppression of Radicals, 1903–1933* (Cambridge: Harvard University Press, 1963), 208–37.

54. Post, *supra* note 53, at 307.

55. See Post, *supra* note 53 at 167 (estimating that approximately six thousand arrest warrants were issued and approximately four thousand warrants executed); Preston, *supra* note 53 at 221 (estimating ten thousand arrests). Many aliens were arrested without warrants. Post, *supra* note 53 at 96, 111; Preston, *supra* note 53, at 221.

56. Murray, *supra* note 53, at 211; see also Preston, *supra* note 53, at 214–18. Prior to December 31, 1919, Rule 22, which governed immigration hearings, provided that: "At the beginning of the hearing under the warrant of arrest the alien shall be allowed to inspect the warrant of arrest and all evidence on which it was issued, and shall be apprised that he may be represented by counsel." Constantine M. Panunzio, *The Deportation Cases of 1919–1920* (New York: Commission on the Church and Social Services, Federal Council of the Churches of Christ in America, 1921), 37. As amended that day, the rule read: "Preferably at the beginning of the hearing under the warrant of arrest or at any rate as soon as such hearing has proceeded sufficiently in the development of the facts to protect the Government's interests, the alien shall be allowed to inspect the warrant of arrest and all the evidence on which it was issued and shall be apprised that thereafter he may be represented by counsel." *Id.*

57. Post, *supra* note 53, at 167.

58. *Id.* at 192.

59. Robert D. Warth, "The Palmer Raids," *South Atlantic Quarterly* 48 (1949): 1, 18.

60. See *Fong Yue Ting v. United States,* 149 U.S. 698 (1893) (holding that deportation is not punishment and does not require the protections of the criminal process).

61. 8 U.S.C. § 1229a(b)(4)(A) (2000) (declaring a statutory right to counsel "at no expense to the Government"); *Aguilera-Enriquez v. INS,* 516 F.2d 565, 568–69 (6th Cir. 1975) (holding that an indigent individual has no constitutional right to counsel in deportation hearings and that counsel must be provided only if necessary to fundamental fairness under due process). Congress has forbidden legal services attorneys from representing any aliens other than lawful permanent residents. See Omnibus Consolidated Rescissions and Appropriations Act of 1996, Pub. L. No. 104–134, § 504(a)(11), 110 Stat. 1321 (prohibiting the use of Legal Service Corporation funding for unlawful aliens).

62. See generally David Cole, "Secrecy, Guilt by Association, and the Terrorist Profile," *Journal of Law and Religion* 15 (2000–2001): 267 (discussing the use of secret evidence in immigration proceedings).

63. See *Yamataya v. Fisher,* 189 U.S. 86 (1903) (holding that aliens are entitled to due process in proceedings to expel them).

64. See Select Comm. to Study Governmental Operations with Respect to Intelligence Activities, Supplementary Detailed Staff Reports on Intelligence Activities and the Rights of Americans (Book III), S. Rep. No. 94–755, at 438–39

(1976) [hereinafter Church Committee Staff Reports]. For an excellent summary of the detention program, see Robert Justin Goldstein, "An American Gulag? Summary Arrest and Emergency Detention of Political Dissidents in the United States," *Columbia Human Rights Law Review* 10 (1978): 541, 558–61.

65. See generally Church Committee Staff Reports, *supra* note 64, at 438–41; Intelligence Activities (vol. 6): Hearings before the Senate Select Comm. to Study Governmental Operations with Respect to Intelligence Activities, 94th Cong. 416–26 (1975) (Exhibit 26–1, Department of Justice memorandum regarding "Program for Apprehension and Detention of Persons Considered Potentially Dangerous to the National Defense and Safety of the United States"); id. at 658–65 (Exhibits 60–3 to -6, regarding Department of Justice "Emergency Detention Program," including model warrants).

66. Act of Sept. 25, 1971, Pub. L. No. 92–128, § 2, 85 Stat. 347.

67. Richard Longaker, "Emergency Detention: The Generation Gap, 1950–71," *Western Political Quarterly* 27 (1974): 395, 402.

68. Wiecek, *supra* note 16, at 427.

69. Church Committee Staff Reports, *supra* note 64, at 441, 445–46.

70. See Robert Goldstein, *Political Repression in Modern America from 1870 to 1976* (Boston: G. K. Hall, 1978), 419.

71. Church Committee Staff Reports, *supra* note 64, at 509–18.

72. 18 U.S.C. § 4001(a) (2000).

73. Goldstein, *supra* note 64, at 572.

74. Brown, *supra* note 1, at 5–7; Bontecou, *supra* note 17.

75. See *Bailey v. Richardson,* 182 F.2d 46, 57–58 (D.C. Cir. 1950), *aff'd by an equally divided court,* 341 U.S. 918 (1951).

76. See generally Alan Barth, *The Loyalty of Free Men* (New York: Viking Press, 1951), 111–14.

77. *Bailey,* 182 F.2d at 66 (Edgerton, J., dissenting).

78. See *id.* at 58.

79. See Laura Kalman, *Abe Fortas: A Biography* (New Haven: Yale University Press, 1990), 137–41. See generally Thurman Arnold, *Fair Fights and Foul: A Dissenting Lawyer's Life* (New York: Harcourt, Brace, and World, 1965), 206–8.

80. See Brown, *supra* note 1, at 181–82.

81. Michael Linfield, *Freedom under Fire: U.S. Civil Liberties in Times of War* (Boston: South End Press, 1990), 86–87.

82. Barth, *supra* note 76, at 62.

83. See Barth, *supra* note 76, at 64–66 (discussing Hollywood's blacklisting of individuals who refused to testify before HUAC); Ellen Schrecker, *Many Are the Crimes: McCarthyism in America* (Boston: Little, Brown, 1998), xiv–xvi.

84. Barth, *supra* note 76, at 10–11.

85. See "Nat'l Popular Gov't League, Report upon the Illegal Practices of the United States Department of Justice" (1920) (authored by R. G. Brown, Zechariah Chafee Jr., Felix Frankfurter, Ernst Freund, Swinburne Hale, Francis Fisher Kane, Alfred S. Niles, Roscoe Pound, Jackson H. Ralston, David Wallerstein, Frank P. Walsh, and Tyrrell Williams).

86. At a recent American Bar Association panel on which I appeared, a Jus-

tice Department official objected to the characterization of the enemy combatants' detention as "incommunicado," pointing out that the detainees are allowed visits from the International Red Cross. But that is about it. Those held as enemy combatants are not permitted phone calls, visits, or contact with anyone outside the military other than the International Red Cross and, on occasion, a diplomatic mission. They are permitted to send and receive only highly censored personal mail. They are kept in their cells for all but thirty minutes a week, unless taken out for interrogation. And they cannot consult a lawyer. See Joseph Lelyveld, "In Guantánamo," *New York Review of Books,* Nov. 7, 2002, 62.

87. Lelyveld, *supra* note 86, at 63.

88. See *Coalition of Clergy v. Bush,* 189 F. Supp. 2d 1036, 1048 (C.D. Cal. 2002), *aff'd in part and vacated in part,* 310 F.3d 1153 (9th Cir. 2002), *cert. denied,* 123 S.Ct. 2073 (2003) (vacating the district court's broad holding that detainees do not have rights to habeas corpus review under any circumstances, but upholding the finding that the petitioners in this case lacked standing); *Rasul v. Bush,* 215 F. Supp. 2d 55, 72–73 (D.D.C. 2002), aff'd, *Al Odab v. United States,* 321 F.3d 1134 (D.C. Cir. 2003), *cert. granted,* 124 S.Ct. 534; but see *Gherebi v. Bush,* 352 F.3d 1278 (9th Cir. 2003).

89. *Hamdi v. Rumsfeld,* 296 F.3d 278, 283 (4th Cir. 2002).

90. While the Fourth Circuit has implied that some review is appropriate, it has also gone out of its way to insist that whatever review is undertaken must be highly deferential: "If dismissal is thus not appropriate, deference to the political branches certainly is. It should be clear that circumspection is required if the judiciary is to maintain its proper posture of restraint. . . . The federal courts have many strengths, but the conduct of combat operations has been left to others. The executive is best . . . prepared to exercise the military judgment attending the capture of alleged combatants. . . . The unconventional aspects of the present struggle do not make its stakes any less grave. Accordingly, any judicial inquiry into Hamdi's status as an alleged enemy combatant in Afghanistan must reflect a recognition that government has no more profound responsibility than the protection of Americans, both military and civilian, against additional unprovoked attack." *Id.*

91. *Hamdi v. Rumsfeld,* 124 S.Ct. 2633 (2004); *Rasul v. Bush,* 124 S.Ct. 2686 (2004).

92. John Ashcroft, Prepared Remarks for the U.S. Mayors Conference (Oct. 25, 2001), available at http://www.usdoj.gov/ag/speeches/2001/agcrisis remarks10_25.htm ("Taking suspected terrorists in violation of the law off the streets and keeping them locked up is our clear strategy to prevent terrorism within our boarders"); see also John Ashcroft, Remarks, Attorney General Ashcroft Outlines Foreign Terrorist Tracking Task Force (Oct. 31, 2001) (transcript available at http://www.usdjo.gov/ag/speeches/2001/agcrisis remarks10_31.htm).

93. See Dan Eggen and Susan Schmidt, "Count of Released Detainees Is Hard to Pin Down," *Washington Post,* Nov. 6, 2001, A10 (reporting a Department of Justice source who stated that 1,182 people had been detained); see also Matthew Brzezinski, "Hady Hassan Omar's Detention," *New York Times,* Oct.

27, 2002, § 6 (magazine), 50 (reporting 1,147 detainees in November 2001); Todd S. Purdum, "Ashcroft's About-Face on the Detainees," *New York Times*, Nov. 28, 2001, B7 (reporting over 1,100 detained).

94. See Amy Goldstein and Dan Eggen, "U.S. to Stop Issuing Detention Tallies," *Washington Post*, Nov. 9, 2001, A16; Purdum, *supra* note 93.

95. See David Cole, *Enemy Aliens: Double Standards and Constitutional Freedoms in the War on Terrorism* (New Press, 2003), 24–26.

96. See generally Cole, *supra* note 52, at 960–65; Human Rights Watch, *Presumption of Guilt: Human Rights Abuses of Post-September 11 Detainees* (2002), available at http://www.hrw.org/reports/2002/us911/USA0802.pdf.

97. See *Detroit Free Press v. Ashcroft*, 303 F.3d 681 (6th Cir. 2002); *North Jersey Media Group, Inc. v. Ashcroft*, 308 F.3d 198 (3d Cir. 2002).

98. See Amnesty Int'l, *Amnesty International's Concerns Regarding Post September 11 Detentions in the USA* (2002), available at http://www.amnestyusa.org/usacrisis/9.11.detentions2.pdf.

99. See Lawyers' Committee for Human Rights, *A Year of Loss: Reexamining Civil Liberties since September 11*, at 19 n.93 (2002), available at http://www.lchr.org/us_law/loss/loss_report.pdf.

100. See Christopher Drew and Judith Miller, "Though Not Linked to Terrorism, Many Detainees Cannot Go Home," *New York Times*, Feb. 18, 2002, A1; see also Class Action Complaint and Demand for Jury Trial, *Turkmen v. Ashcroft*, CV-02-307 (E.D.N.Y. 2002), available at http://news.findlaw.com/hdocs/docs/terrorism/turkmenash41702cmp.pdf; Susan Sachs, "Civil Rights Group to Sue over U.S. Handling of Muslim Men," *New York Times*, Apr. 17, 2002, A13.

101. See Danny Hakim, "Four Are Charged with Belonging to a Terror Cell," *New York Times*, Aug. 29, 2002, A1 (reporting that three of the four men charged as part of a Detroit terror cell were initially arrested during post–September 11 preventive detention sweeps); Kirk Semple, "Sumali is Indicted for Alleged Plot in Ohio," *New York Times*, June 14, 2004 (reporting on terrorist indictment of a foriegn national held initially on immigration charges).

102. See Danny Hakim, "Two Arabs Convicted and 2 Cleared of Terrorist Plot against the U.S.," *New York Times*, June 4, 2003, A21; Hakim, "Inquiries Begun into Handling of Detroit Terror Cases," *New York Times*, Jan. 29, 2004, A23. One of the two men tried and convicted was not the subject of preventive detention, but was arrested only after charges were filed. The other three were intially swept up in the post–September 11 round-up.

103. John Ashcroft, Remarks at the U.S. Attorneys Conference (Oct. 1, 2002), available at http://www.justice.gov/ag/speeches/2002/100102agremarkstousattorneysconference.htm; see Lawyers' Committee for Human Rights, *supra* note 99, at 27 n.72 (citing Letter from Daniel J. Bryant, Assistant Attorney General, U.S. Department of Justice, to Senator Carl Levin, Chairman of Permanent Subcommittee on Investigations, Senate Committee on Governmental Affairs (July 3, 2002)).

104. 150 U.S.C. § 1701(a) (2000).

105. Exec. Order No. 12,947, 3 C.F.R. 319 (1995), reprinted in 50 U.S.C. § 1701 (2000).

106. *Id.* § 1(a)(iii).

107. Exec. Order No. 13,224 § 1(d), 3 C.F.R. 786, (2001), reprinted in 50 U.S.C.A § 1701 (West Supp. 2002).

108. See Uniting and Strengthening America by Providing Appropriate Tools Required to Intercept and Obstruct Terrorism (USAPATRIOT) Act of 2001, Pub. L. No. 107–56, § 106, 115 Stat. 272, 277–78 (amending 50 U.S.C. § 1702(a)(1)(B) and adding 50 U.S.C. § 1702(c)).

109. See *Global Relief Found. v. O'Neill,* 207 F. Supp. 2d 779 (N.D. Ill. 2002), aff'd, 315 F.3d 748 (7th Cir. 2002), *cert. denied,* 124 S.Ct. 531 (2003); *Holy Land Found. for Relief & Dev. v. Ashcroft,* 219 F. Supp. 2d 57 (D.D.C. 2002), aff'd, 333 F.3d 156 (D.C. Cir. 2003), *cert. denied,* 124 S.Ct. 1506 (2004).

110. See David Johnston, "U.S. Prosecutors Suspect an American Citizen of Financing Hamas Terror," *New York Times,* June 14, 1998, A20.

111. List of Specially Designated Terrorists Who Threaten to Disrupt the Middle East Peace Process, 60 Fed. Reg. 41,152 (Aug. 11, 1995).

112. See Johnston, *supra* note 110; Ashraf Kalil, "U.S. Citizen Accused by Israel of Having Hamas Ties Becomes Test Case for Arab-Americans and Israeli Justice System," *Cairo Times,* Aug. 6–10, 1998, 11.

113. Oren Gross, "Cutting Down Trees: Law-Making under the Shadow of Great Calamities," in *The Security of Freedom: Essays on Canada's Anti-Terrorism Bill,* ed. Ronald Daniels et al. (Toronto: University of Toronto Press, 2001), 39.

114. *Id.* at 40–42.

115. See Dana Milbank, "Opinion of U.S. Abroad Is Falling, Survey Finds," *Washington Post,* Mar. 17, 2004; see also, Raymond Bonner, "Southeast Asia Remains Fertile for Al-Qaeda," *New York Times,* Oct. 28, 2002, A1; Frank Bruni, "Europe Pauses and Grieves, but Takes Issue With U.S.," *New York Times,* Sept. 12, 2002, B1; Zbigniew Brzezinski, "Confronting Anti-American Grievances," *New York Times,* Sept. 1, 2002, § 4, 9; Thomas Friedman, "Tone It Down a Notch," *New York Times,* Oct. 2, 2002, A27; Neil MacFarquhar, "Threats and Responses: Security; For Americans in Mideast, Daily Balance of Risk," *New York Times,* Oct. 31, 2002, A12; Craig S. Smith, "Saved by U.S., Kuwait Now Shows Mixed Feelings," *New York Times,* Oct. 12, 2002, A11.

CONSTITUTIONAL REASON OF STATE: THE FEAR FACTOR

Nancy L. Rosenblum

INTRODUCTION: "NECESSITY" & POLITICAL JUDGMENT

Like regimes throughout history, contemporary constitutional democracies face periodic threats to their security. These threats come from internal and external enemies—subversives and armed combatants, civilian and military—employing every imaginable means of attack, from the exploitation of electoral politics by enemies of democracy to violent terrorism. Estimates of the nature and requirements of "security" always vary, as do assessments of the threat and of what is necessary for effective self-protection. One thing is constant. Governments will wield all their resources in response to threats: police and law enforcement, emergency legislation, executive orders, ordinary and extraordinary tribunals, military mobilization. And these responses will test constitutional constraints: the jurisdiction of political authorities, their powers, and the civil liberties of citizens from speech rights to established rules of criminal due process. By definition, "constitutionalism is a precommitment to adhere to rules of restraint in the long term no matter how great the temptation to depart from them in the short term on grounds of social utility."[1] Ranged against this is the countervailing force of Bassiano's plea to the Duke in *The Merchant of Venice* to void Shylock's contract: "To do a great right, do a little wrong."

In the history of political thought, the idea of "reason of state" captures this tension between legal constraints and grim necessity. It gives a name to our subject. It is shorthand for the dilemma of security and protection, loyalty and dissent, in dangerous times. *Reason of state* refers to the measures required for political survival—the deep necessities of preservation. The newly minted "Office of Homeland Security" suggests physical safety within geographic boundaries—up to the water's edge. But constitutional reason of state presents a distinctive dilemma because it is also about the political *character* of society as expressed in its basic institutions and practices. Survival of constitutional order is at stake, not order simply: a government of limited powers designed to serve substantive ends—personal freedom or political participation.

In all this, the worthiness of the political order is assumed, making its preservation the responsibility of governors and making reason of state an articulable *political* morality.[2] An additional assumption is that the measures required *will* violate to some extent the moral norms and legal rules that ordinarily constrain political action. The question is how much deviation can be sustained without altering the character of the regime. "In every government, there must be somewhat fundamental, somewhat like a *Magna Charta,* that should be standing and unalterable."[3] How much deviation and what derogation, in what contexts and in regard to how many citizens, or what classes of citizens (or noncitizens), can occur without undermining *our* constitutional order? This is Aristotle's question: when can we say that one regime has changed into another—democracy into tyranny, for example?[4]

The dilemma of reason of state is irreducible, at least so long as we reject *fiat justicia pereat mundus.* Jefferson rejected it: "A strict observance of the written laws is doubtless one of the high duties of a good citizen, but it is not the highest. The laws of necessity, of self-preservation, of saving our country when in danger, are of higher obligation."[5] President Lincoln rejected *fiat justicia* too, as responsible leaders always have: "Every government when driven to the wall by a rebellion will trample down a constitution before it will allow itself to be destroyed. This may not be constitutional law but it is a fact."[6] We are retrospectively resigned to Lincoln's judgment because of the justice of his cause. But the question whether "necessity" required suspending the writ of habeas corpus and civilian courts is still contested.

"Necessity may know no law," but there is no science of necessity.

Calculating sufficient means—estimating what is required but no more than is required for security (an "economy of violence")—is a matter of probabilities, something of a wager, entailing an element of prophecy. Public announcements of "vague but credible threats" and the familiar designation "security risk" capture this uncertainty. Feelings of insecurity are not well tied to measures of the extent of the danger. There are always too many targets, and too many resources for attacking them. The strange term *intelligence* is a justification for gathering information and a virtual admission of its tentativeness and incompleteness; as one expert puts it, "Intelligence is a game of strategy played by competitors."[7] There are no *arcana imperii*—though officials often pretend the contrary and claim to know what others cannot: the imminence of danger, the identity and designs of the enemy, their motivations and tactics and organization or "networks." Secrecy reinforces governors' status as privileged interpreters of necessity: classified information, executive privilege, direct or indirect restrictions on speech and press, surveillance, selective and indeterminate detentions. Recent American history offers examples: the "secret war" in Laos kept from Congress and public scrutiny from 1962 through 1969 for reasons that had little to do with the military need for clandestine operations (the *enemy* knew we were bombing, after all); the secret parallel government created to organize national security operations in the Iran-Contra affair. Political authorities exploit security threats and popular insecurity to exercise powers they would not otherwise possess and that would not normally be tolerated, at least not without substantial dissent.

But the problem at the root of reason of state remains, even if governors are not seeking dictatorial power and do not exploit the occasion to target their political opponents; it is an ineliminable element of political life in dangerous times. Governors ask for (and generally receive) the greatest trust at the moment they should be most mistrusted, because they more than anyone are motivated to take an opportunistic view of necessity. Nothing is more likely to dampen deliberation than "emergency," or more likely to weaken success at getting the information necessary for a democratic public to be confident that the measures justified as necessary really are.

In the first part of this essay I offer a typology of accounts of constitutional reason of state designed to point up the "exceptionalism" of American constitutionalism in grappling with the demands of reason of state. I then consider extraconstitutional political constraints that temper the predictable illiberalism of government during dangerous times. In the final section I consider the "fear factor." Fear is a key element of reason of state. It is an opening for extended powers. It can also motivate vigilance against abuse of power. My main point, however, is to challenge the orthodoxy that fear is "the passion to be reckoned with" when security is at stake. It does not stand alone. Another emotional force drives protective and retaliatory action, and is always on the brink of slipping into evil. Fear's passionate counterpart is the visceral excitation of direct, vengeful action outside and against the law.

THREE MODELS OF CONSTITUTIONAL REASON OF STATE

One theory of reason of state owes to Machiavelli and his heirs among republican theorists. Not the Machiavelli of *The Prince,*who insisted that rulers must learn how not to be good (though this too is relevant to reason of state—rulers must *learn* now not to be good because not being good *well* is difficult). Rather, the powerful voice here is Machiavelli of the *Discourses on Livy,* who studied the assignment of extraordinary power in the Roman Republic and advised that "all republics should have some institution similar to the dictatorship."[8] In Rome, in response to a concrete emergency, power was given to one man to make decisions without consultation and to execute them without appeal. He was a constitutional dictator, not a tyrant, because his power was circumscribed by law. Dictatorship was a separate office: the dictator was elected by petition of the senate to the consuls (when *they* not he determined the necessity); for a limited time (six months); for an assigned commission (such as suppressing rebellion); within specified limits (the dictator could not alter existing law or create new law). His job was to make himself superfluous, like Cincinnatus, returning to his fields. The important point is that no dictator could assume authority on his own authority. This is the very opposite of Carl Schmitt's pronouncement: "Sovereign is he who decides on the exception."[9]

Machiavelli's reason of state is compatible with *constitutional* bases for exceptions as long as they are not self-executing or self-limiting. Today, many constitutions, including India's and South Africa's, incorporate emergency power clauses prescribing arrangements to meet crises and at the same time specifying certain nonderogable rights.[10] Constitutional theorists have advocated a version of Roman constitutional dictatorship for the United States. They argue that constitutionally facilitated emergency power requires a formal declaration of emergency and the explicit assumption of powers to meet it. On this view, constitutionalizing emergency power puts pressure on authorities to give public reasons. It is said to enhance accountability. Perhaps the chief merit is that constitutionally prescribed emergency power designates a normal institution to decide that an exceptional situation exists, so that reason of state has external authorization. Clinton Rossiter, who argued that the institution of a temporary presidential dictatorship exists de facto in the United States and should be formally acknowledged, was disturbed by the absence of external authorization of "necessity" in practice.[11] Consider by way of example this oral argument in the district court case leading up to *Youngstown* (1952).[12] In the face of labor unrest President Truman proposed to take over the steel industry to avert a wartime crisis of production.

> *Court:* Then, as I understand it, you claim that in time of emergency the Executive has this great power.
> *Mr. Baldridge:* That is correct.
> *Court:* And that the Executive determines the emergencies and the Courts cannot even review whether it is an emergency.
> *Mr. Baldridge:* That is correct.

This posture is distinguishable from the related but more extreme position taken by President Nixon: "When the President does it, that means that it is not illegal."[13]

A second tradition of reason of state can be traced to John Locke in chapter 14 of his *Second Treatise of Government*, where this severe constitutionalist concedes that accidents and necessities arise that the law cannot anticipate and for which it cannot prescribe. What is required is prerogative power. The prerogative is discretionary power exercised by the executive outside and against the law. But prerogative is limited rather than broadly permissive. The idea is one of antilegal measures that are discrete, measured, and justifiable in terms accessible to people generally. In Locke's familiar formula, prerogative is "the power of doing public good without a rule."

In Locke, as in Machiavelli, we have straightforward recognition that adherence to law may do irreparable harm. We also have straightforward recognition that officials will always self-righteously identify what they do with the public good. What protection is there, then, against the protective device of prerogative discretion? In the same chapter of the *Second Treatise* in which he discusses prerogative power, Locke introduces his theory of revolution. A popular "appeal to heaven" is his answer to abuse: "If there comes to be a question between the executive power and the people about a thing claimed as a prerogative, the tendency of the exercise of such prerogative to the good or hurt of the people will easily decide that question."[14] The counterweight to prerogative is political resistance. The people generally must feel the abuse and be wary of it and think it necessary to put an end to it.

Prerogative is a live idea for those who contend that extralegal national security measures are safer than seeking a constitutional warrant for setting aside the usual protections for rights and liberties.[15] The argument is that legalization of extralegal means permanently distorts constitutionalism. It sets dangerous precedents. When the U.S. Supreme Court justifies extraordinary national security measures as constitutional business-as-usual, its authority as interpreter of rights and powers is corroded. The Court is famously deferential to presidential power during wartime and other national security emergencies, provoking a picture of the Court "beating a unanimous retreat to the fortress of technicality" or handing down a "stately parade of judicial clichés."[16] Justice Jackson's dissent in *Korematsu* argued against providing a constitutional warrant for emergency powers that violate rights and the separation of powers. He made the case for the frankly extralegal exercise of prerogative power.

> A judicial construction of the due process clause that will sustain this order is a far more subtle blow to liberty than the promulgation of the order itself. A military order, however, unconstitutional, is not apt to last longer than the military emergency. . . . But once a judicial opinion rationalizes such an order to show that it conforms to the Constitution, or rather rationalizes the Constitution to show that the Constitution sanctions such an order, the court for all time has validated the principle of racial discrimination in criminal procedure and of transplanting American citizens.[17]

(It is worth noting that the *Korematsu* decision has not been overruled, and is cited, bizarrely, as a protoprecedent for strict scrutiny of racial classifications!)

Perhaps the most important argument advanced by advocates of prerogative is the echo of Locke's view that finally the check on prerogative power is popular political resistance. Where action for the public good is taken without legal warrant, the argument goes, attention is rightly drawn to the fact that reason of state entails *political* not legal judgment and that our recourse in the event of abuse of power is *political* opposition (that is, censure, or impeachment, or civil disobedience, or organized resistance).

Comparative constitutionalism exhibits many variations on constitutional dictatorship and prerogative, among them emergency powers, designated war powers and martial law, and a legally determined state of siege, along with various mechanisms for formal authorization and review. It is a mark of American exceptionalism to insist on constitutional continuity between dangerous times, including wartime, and presumably peaceful normal times. The Constitution was adopted in a period of grave emergency. "The Constitution of the U.S. is a law for rulers and people, equally in war and peace," and "no doctrine involving more pernicious consequences was ever invented by the wit of man than that any of its provisions can be suspended during any of the great exigencies of government."[18] On this view, the Constitution suffices for determining what is permissible during emergencies as well as business-as-usual. Actions are seen as law-bound; the discretionary is disallowed even as a "troubling exception."[19] There is one unified constitutional system, not one for normal and one for exceptional times.

This means that exceptional actions to meet emergencies take the usual forms: administrative orders or legislative action. Congress has passed myriads of statutes authorizing executive action to meet new dangers (the Tonkin Gulf resolution) and adding to the powers of the executive branch (the post-9/11 USA Patriot Act), creating new agencies like the Department of Homeland Security and expanding law-enforcement authority. Congress, then, does not just defer to the exercise of presidential authority during times of crisis, but materially enhances it. I will return in a moment to the question whether legislatively created emergency powers provide a check on the executive, as separation of powers suggests, and whether these measures are temporary, as is often supposed, or result in permanent institutional change. The important point is the operative assumption that these changes—whether taken by the president alone or authorized by the legislature—are compatible with the Constitution and with constitutional safeguards and constraints normally understood. They are exceptional measures to meet exceptional times, but they do not alter or deviate from normal constitutionalism. These measures are subject to judicial review after the fact. "Constitutional continuity" remains the rule.

We have examples of constitutional continuity guaranteed by courts that judged an assumption of power or infringement of rights impermissible—at least after the fact.[20] President Lincoln's suspension of the writ of habeas corpus was ruled unconstitutional by the Supreme Court; Article I, section 9 suggests that the writ can be suspended ("unless when in cases of rebellion or invasion the public safety may require it"), but that only Congress has that power. Similarly, the right to civil judicial processes was upheld ("martial law can never exist where the courts are open, and in the proper and unobstructed exercise of their jurisdiction").[21] In a rare, effective (rather than ex post) upholding of constitutional constraints on the executive during wartime the Supreme Court denied President Truman authority to seize the steel mills, on grounds that the "theatre of war" does not expand to include labor disputes.[22] This prohibition on an extraordinary exercise of power by a president during war is the exception. Commentators suggest the result owed to the fact that the right at stake was corporate private property. It concedes a fluid rather than bright-line approach to presidential authority.

This theory of constitutional continuity, of a seamless fabric uninterrupted by reason of state, has not meant invariable protection of liberties or constraints on government. Constitutional interpretation typically defers to presidents. The practical implication of this view—"while the Constitution protects against invasions of individual rights, it is not a suicide pact"[23]—has not been *suspension* of constitutional protections but rather *interpreting* them to permit (what are later ruled) violations of basic rights. Put succinctly, the constitution is "invariant between war and peacetime but . . . emergency conditions tip the balance of security and liberty differently in either circumstance."[24] In short, justices have taken the view that the Constitution provides for executive power to meet perceived emergencies. And the Court has declined to independently examine whether an emergency is present. Thus, the Supreme Court upheld convictions under the World War I Espionage and Sedition Acts for acts including distributing leaflets to draftees that declared conscription to be slavery.[25] The most egregious case was the relocation and internment of 120,000 West Coast citizens and residents of Japanese descent during World War II. While detention constituted discrimination based on race or ancestry, the Court acknowledged, it was justified by "the judgment of the military authorities and of Congress that there were disloyal members" among Japanese Americans and that "in a critical hour such persons could not readily be isolated and separately dealt with."[26] After Pearl Harbor Roosevelt announced, "We will not, under any threat, or in the face of any danger, surrender the guarantees of liberty our forefathers framed for us in our Bill of Rights." But it should come as no surprise that when he considered Japanese internment he was not plagued by the constitutional difficulty. "The Constitution has not greatly bothered any wartime President."[27]

Undoubtedly, recent infringements on civil liberties and exercises of executive authority after the terrorist attacks of September 11, 2001, and the two wars that followed will eventually be tested in court. Among them are infringements of rights to privacy (including privileged communications with legal counsel) and habeas corpus and the collapse of the distinction between domestic criminal surveillance (subject to Fourth Amendment requirements) and surveillance of foreign governments and agents. Morton Halperin's observation that "the government has often believed that anyone who is protesting government policy is doing it at the behest of a foreign government and opened counterintelligence investigations of them"[28] becomes more salient with the official collapse of the distinction between internal and external security, domestic and foreign surveillance, intelligence gathering and gathering evidence for criminal prosecution. Also contested is the blurring of the constitutional separation between the domains of civilian and military authority (federal troops in airports, most visibly) and the assignment of increased powers to public health and immigration authorities (expanding their discretion, granting broad power to classify information as secret, and turning them into tools of law enforcement and agents of the national security apparatus).[29] The challenges will come in legal venues not political ones. This lengthy process of litigation is significant because cases are reviewed one by one. There is no occasion or obligation to assess the totality of consequences for American constitutional identity. Moreover, judicial review of the question whether violations of civil liberties have occurred does not address the nonlegal question whether the violations are justifiable. Legal challenges divert attention from independent political assessments of "necessity." In dangerous times, when the authority and justification of action depends on defining a threat and measures to meet it, "government by lawsuit becomes unthinkable."[30]

Proponents of American "continuous constitutionalism" are not blind to judicial deference to political authorities during dangerous times or to the precedents created. One sanguine defense of this model argues that over time the invocation of constitutional constraints in response to emergency powers fosters an enhanced public constitutional consciousness. It encourages vigilant not tranquilized responses. Supporters are confident that American constitutional identity as pronounced by courts is progressive, even as regards reason of state. Justice Brennan expressed this view in a talk at Hebrew University in 1987. He appealed to a maturing theory of the Bill of Rights, a slow accumulation of liberty-protective precedents, and lessons that have been learned from "sustained exposure to so-called security threats."[31]

Can any generalizations be made about the comparative politics of these three models of reason of state or about the tendency of one or another approach to reason of state to strike the most dependable or reasonable between liberty and security? Machiavelli's Roman dictatorship, Locke's prerogative power, and American continuous constitutionalism all have the formal capacity to constrain political authorities—to set limits to what reason of state permits. They are also equally capable of licensing what has been called a "dual state,"[32] that is, a political order in which the normal rule of law operates in most areas of life but is suspended (or reinterpreted) in some domains. In the dual state, the dominance of civilian authorities is weakened, the jurisdictions that separate civilian from military authority are blurred, and special institutions are created.[33]

One key feature of a dual state is that certain groups are classed as dangerously subversive or enemies of the state—communists, Jews, homosexuals, racially profiled immigrants—and receive differential treatment by law enforcement, regulatory authorities (the INS, for example), and courts, a point emphasized by David Cole and Katherine Franke in their contributions to this volume. A regular casualty of security crises is the subversion of an essential element of legalism with the turn from "individualized suspicion" to group profiling. The issue of civil liberties frequently devolves into an issue of targeting. A group's associations and practices may be criminalized; the USA Patriot Act gives the secretary of state authority (without review) to designate any group, foreign or domestic, a terrorist organization. This egregious deviation from the norm of individual responsibility effectively designates groups outlaws regardless of any specific violations of the law. Reason of state justifies depriving members of their constitutional rights—indeed of their status as citizens or their status as combatants under treaties—making them vulnerable to exile or imprisonment or detention in camps. A version of "outlawing" occurs when government characterizes the attacks on the Pentagon and World Trade Center as neither a crime nor an act of war. The decision not to apply the Bill of Rights to noncitizen suspects (or detainees no longer suspect) in the recent attacks does not go to the limit (it may not even be unconstitutional), but it is justified by reason of state and alerts us to its dangerous mechanisms and plain cruelty.

Every form of constitutional reason of state—constitutional arrangements providing for emergency powers, extraconstitutional prerogative, and constitutional business-as-usual—has its critics and defenders. Carl Friedrich's comparative study of constitutional democracies in practice was inconclusive. Comparative politics reveals the variability of institutional arrangements for addressing national security, but Friedrich could find no reason for preferring one over another as more effective in meeting national security threats on the one hand or more solicitous of constitutional limits and civil liberties on the other. "Until now," he cautioned, "those constitutional systems which survived did so not because they had solved the problem of internal security but because the problem never became sufficiently serious in the liberal age to threaten the existence of these states."[34]

Friedrich reminds us that the United States has not had to deal with strong internal enemies of constitutional democracy—with effective political parties that exploit electoral politics to gain power in order to subvert democracy, or violent internal factions threatening civil war, or shattering domestic upheavals, or subversives who pose a real "clear and present danger," or clandestine agents of terror or foreign conquest. Friedrich had the contrast with Weimar Germany in mind: "When confronted with the real threat of Communist conquest, the bourgeoisie, so-called, has typically reacted by becoming Fascist."[35] The American theory of constitutional continuity has been a thin restraint on reason of state in practice, but the dangers, too, have been weak. It is easier to advocate civil liberties absolutism or constitutional business-as-usual when the historical record is one of "silly leaflets" handed out by "poor and puny anonymities" (Holmes's and Brandeis's characterizations of anarchists), McCarthyism aimed at Hollywood screenwriters, the internment of Japanese Americans, or surveillance and harassment of Vietnam War protestors (and anyone else who caught the security agencies' attention, or, we now know, agents' prurient interest). The problem of reason of state challenges even strong civil libertarians after the experience of large-scale violent terrorism that took advantage of American openness and made the idea of more and more dangerous attacks plausible.

I am not aware of any systematic consideration of whether constitutional arrangements make a difference in how risks to security are calculated or in solicitude for the rights and liberties of men and women personally or as members of targeted groups. In part this comparative politics is difficult because it requires generalizations among regimes or across emergencies faced by a single regime under conditions defined from the start as extraordinary, not ordinary.

In any case, comparison is not decisive because constitutional arrangements are not what principally matters in explaining patterns of decisions when it comes to expulsion of aliens, court martial jurisdiction over civilians, loyalty programs, wiretaps, revocation of passports, detention of suspects, and devolution to a "dual state." If formal constitutionalism and doctrinal criteria for balancing security against liberty are not decisive, what is?

TEMPERING "NECESSITY": EXTRACONSTITUTIONAL CONSTRAINTS DURING DANGEROUS TIMES

One answer to the question whether extraconstitutional constraints can be effective is impracticable but deserves mention because it is often invoked. I refer to the notion that the United States can avoid danger and the threats to liberty that arise from security crises by taking advantage of its natural insularity. The warning against foreign entanglements is as old as the republic. It arises again and again; whether it takes the form of isolationism or modest internationalism, the idea is that the nation brings security crises, with their physical danger and danger to liberty, on itself. Arthur Schlesinger, for example, argued that the only way to preserve liberty at home was to abandon "messianic" foreign policies. It is because the United States acts as a global superpower that it is vulnerable to foreign aggression. More important, aggressive foreign policy infects domestic policy and strains constitutionalism, upsetting the balance of powers by aggrandizing presidents and bypassing Congress and courts. A rational, responsible, discriminating internationalism is Schlesinger's solution.[36]

Whether or not the United States provokes violence against itself through overreaching or unjust policies, it is clearly, painfully, vulnerable to mass casualties and undeterrable, "asymmetrical threats." And no attempt to address the "root cause" of anti-Americanism can eliminate the danger. (Besides, nothing is as contested as accounts of motives and grievances: are terrorists driven by religious fanaticism or cultural deracination, or specific American foreign policies, or, least likely as a motivation and least corrigible, economic deprivation?) Security threats cannot be ameliorated in the short run by policy changes, or concessions to radicals, or aid programs aimed at improving economic conditions, or conversion to multilateralism, or efforts at disengagement and energy self-sufficiency. Nor can the United States be made invulnerable by promoting policies that reduce anarchy abroad—by doing what it can to see that foreign governments have the moral legitimacy and material capacity to control dangerous dissidents in their own territory rather than indulge them, covertly support them, or exile them. All this is long-term at best; it does not address immediate threats; it is purely conjectural as to motivation. Modern communication and transportation allow small, autonomous, well-financed, unaccountable groups or "networks," "nonstate actors," paramilitary organizations, suicidally violent young men and women to function, and modern media make the terrorist spectacle just that, which will always have seductive appeal.

There are independent reasons for altering American foreign policy, but they are not principally justified as ways of eradicating the conditions that give rise to enemies or to the conditions invoked by reason of state. Instead, I propose three other extraconstitutional factors that constrain government even in the face of emergencies.

First, whether they rest on constitutional warrant or not, the measures and institutions produced in response to national emergencies have an atomic half-life. The occasion for extended powers may be described as aberrational, but the permit endures. Every scholar of emergency powers documents the fact that these laws are not temporary. Regimes transformed by emergency powers do not return to their "original position." What began as something exceptional becomes normal. In 1974 a Senate committee estimated that more than 470 pieces of emergency legislation in the United States in which Congress delegated discretionary powers to presidents remained on the statute books, and the number has doubtless multiplied since then.[37] One exception is a 1971 law repealing the "mothballing" of detention camps for future use. The Bush Justice Department characterizes the expansion of its legal authority as largely a matter of dusting off little-used powers created during past crises.

Enduring emergency measures are more salient today given the permanent crisis of vulnerability to terrorist attack (though in fact the notion of a perpetual emergency, of an end to "normal times," is not new).[38] Many of the security measures are preventive, not a response to enemy or terrorist actions, and hence lie outside the scope of military action: detentions of citizens or aliens, new designations like "illegal combatants," new forms of surveillance, all lower or eliminate the burden of probable cause ordinarily imposed on government officials, and many are not subject to review by any court or independent party. The measures challenge core elements of American constitutional identity, most obviously blurring of the division between civilian/military and internal/external security. Statements by the assistant attorney general in charge of the Criminal Division of the Justice Department, Michael Chertoff, make this vivid: "In past terrorist investigations, you usually had a defined event and you're investigating after the fact. That's not what we had here. This is not Tim McVeigh. It's not even WTC I where things stabilized after a period of time. We have an organization that never says 'We've done this, we're done. It's the end of the war.'" Chertoff also said, "You can't divide the world any longer into intelligence defense on the one hand and law enforcement on the other. . . .

On September 11th, we realized that we couldn't debate it philosophically anymore."[39]

One extraconstitutional factor constraining runaway reason of state, then, is whether the security threat is viewed as discrete, time-bounded, or space-bound and restricted to a theater of war. If not, if threats are diffuse and open-ended, viewed as more than a crisis, reason of state too slips from extraordinary to ordinary. If measures in response to perceived emergency cannot be cabined, it is the responsibility of political representatives to look beyond the immediate. That is, legislation must take into account the long life-cycle and unanticipated consequences of legal change—the new statutes and adaptive constitutional interpretations—in determining the cost of any response. The USA Patriot Act passed by Congress in 2001 was amended at the insistence of a few civil liberties–conscious Democrats to include a "sunset provision" requiring reconsideration in five years. At present, congressional Republicans are working to amend the act, and any successors, by making the sweeping antiterrorism powers permanent.

A second extraconstitutional factor is Madison's "extent" of political society and its decentralization. The United States is large and politically fragmented. When national security measures are discrete and under federal control, they are more likely to be severe and effective (e.g., presidential seizure of steel mills or Japanese American "relocation"). More often, however, security measures are taken by a ceaselessly multiplying array of federal and state agencies and dispersed local authorities, acting under state as well as federal laws, with variable intents and effects. The Office of Homeland Security promises to share information and coordinate a comprehensive national strategy to secure the United States—to create something closer to a disciplinary state with capillary coverage (or, to avoid hyperbole, to consider merging the Border Patrol, the Customs Service, and the Coast Guard, which resist consolidation). But a certain laxness in centralization of information, coordination, and oversight is inevitable, not only for technical reasons or because the most likely result is system overload, but because it goes against an ingrained American history of political structures and entrenched political interests. Also at work is the plain fact of differential commitments to constitutional constraints, in particular classic First Amendment constraints; both select local police departments and select universities have refused to cooperate with the FBI request to interview and track young Middle Eastern men.

Consider one illustration of political fragmentation in this context. In the few months following September 11, we watched the contest between civil liberties groups and the Justice Department over secret detentions of noncitizens. It appears that early on the attorney general was *exaggerating* the number of detainees for political reasons—he thought it would buck up the public to know that over 1,000 people were being held for questioning. It also appears that, at least initially, the government's inability to produce the actual numbers and disposition of cases was less evasion than disorganization. The Justice Department's count apparently included everyone questioned by local police, but the department did not collect reports about whether or when those rounded up were released. The executive branch of the federal government encourages secrecy; it prohibits state and local governments from making the names of detainees public, for example. But secrecy is also an intragovernmental affair, a matter of territoriality. This is a double-edged sword, of course; it limits accountability and limits unified action.

Size and lack of coordination (and competition) as obstacles to efficient reason of state is also confirmed in the story of Dr. Al Bader al-Hazmi in a *New York Times* report aptly titled "Who is this Kafka that people keep mentioning?" The doctor, an anesthesiology resident from Texas, was taken into custody, didn't see his lawyer for seven days, and didn't get to answer his keepers' questions until day twelve, after which he was quickly cleared. Dr. al-Hazmi reflected: "At the end I said to myself, These guys are clueless. . . . How can they figure out who is behind this thing? I would suggest that Americans don't rely on the FBI. I say, God must protect America instead."[40]

I don't mean to suggest that failure to coordinate is always benign; it can weaken security in critical instances. Nor do I suggest that weak government is good for civil liberties. Personal liberty is dependent on collective security. Constitutional protections are most fragile under governments that lack support for legalism, are unable to control the military and private groups, and are vulnerable to populist demands for exhibitions of aggressive leadership. My point is that a diffuse apparatus, the difficulty of centralization, and "our localism" potentially mitigate rigorously consistent, large-scale incursions on civil liberties. Again, these tempering factors can potentially be overcome by databases, federalizing law enforcement and taking it out of the hands of states and localities, and so on (leaving aside the very important question of centralization of the media and its tendency to self-censorship). But diffuse authority is not just de facto, it is a long tradition that operates to resist efficient and unified execution of "necessary means."

The third and most important extraconstitutional factor constraining government emergency power has to do with the strength of civil society. The current, fashionable civil society literature is preoccupied with trust—meaning horizontal trust among citizens that fosters social cooperation. This "social capital," the argument goes, spills over from religious groups, book clubs, and athletic teams to public life. This benign story has eclipsed the classic political theory focus on civil society as the source of *distrust* and resistance to abuse of power. True, when security is threatened, disaggregated "public opinion" typically mirrors or runs ahead of official estimates of danger and "necessity." But *organized* semipublics, voluntary associations, and advocacy groups do provide scrutiny, demand information, challenge statements of fact and law, and mobilize political opposition.

Critical here are associations dedicated to watchdog functions: scrutiny, publicity, political advocacy, and lobbying as well as selecting, funding, and moving cases challenging the constitutionality of government action through the courts. A prime example is the ACLU, which does not rest (as Amnesty International often must) on Enlightenment faith in publicity; the ACLU takes political action. Between September 11 and the passage of the USA Patriot Act on October 26, the Washington Office generated 15 issue briefs and letters on every version of the bill to congressional staffs, fielded 650 press calls, and generated 15,000 emails and faxes to Congress. It lobbied individual congressmen and women and testified at Patriot Act hearings (which, because they were not called hearings, were not televised on C-SPAN and did not produce official transcripts). The organization can claim some credit for the final bill, which the Bush administration described as a concession to the demands of civil liberties groups. Moreover, the ACLU had up and running an immigrants' rights project that it uses to try to track detainees. It had a project on government profiling via investigation techniques, which has followed and challenged current proposals. These projects are also sources for finding the right plaintiffs and constructing litigation.

Important too are particularist identity groups that protect and speak on behalf of their own. The multiplication of racial, ethnic, and religious groups (among them Arab citizen groups) with resources for organization, mobilization, and response are one factor in government circumspection that the onus of security measures not fall too heavily on vulnerable minorities. For if "war is an aggregation of hardships," from a civil liberty standpoint the hardships are unevenly distributed in predictable ways. The ACLU has been running focus groups. The general response from members has been disappointing; a common posture is, "if I'm not a terrorist they can tap my phone or get at my business records." But African Americans are deeply wary of government power: "They just passed a law and they say they are going to use it for terrorists, but they are going to use it for anyone." Another offered, "You are talking about power and you know that they are going to abuse it. You know who they are going to use it on, us."[41] Organized groups raise the political salience of targeting. We are reminded, however, that advocacy groups are unequal, and that some people are inadequately protected. Immigrants are plainly vulnerable (to say nothing of the thousands of refugees who were cleared to come to the United States and have been indefinitely delayed). They recall to us the human costs of reason of state. Restrictions on liberty in the name of necessity are sometimes general; the burden may be widely shared. But most often restrictions fall on specific, targeted groups. We have seen—*Korematsu* is the classic case—that courts cannot be depended upon to exercise strict scrutiny of denials of equal protection of the law when it comes to incursions on the liberty of racial or ethnic or religious groups under "emergency" conditions. It is even less likely that legislators will serve as brakes on executive action when it is aimed at a selected minority rather than at the population generally. The best defense, in the courts and in the face of legislation, is organized interest and advocacy groups.

To sum up my third point about extraconstitutional constraints on government: politically organized partial publics substitute for Lockean majoritarianism as the source of challenge to "necessity" and resistance to abuse of power. Majoritarianism takes a back seat to pluralism—to the formation of groups whose purpose, directly or indirectly, is self-protection against the overreaching of those charged with judging what is necessary for national self-protection.

THE FEAR FACTOR

Implied by the idea of constitutional reason of state is a constitutional ethos or identity. The importance of extraconstitutional *political* checks on government raises the question, Do Americans identify with an identity that privileges liberties and is skeptical of claims of "necessity"? Is constitutional culture on the minds of democratic citizens and their political representatives? If not, why not?

The temptation to illiberalism during dangerous times is typically charged to fear: both the rational fear that adjusts the balance between liberty and security and the irrational fear that defers to any claim that a measure is necessary for national protection. Fear, the argument goes, overwhelms steady commitment to political restraint. I want to examine this orthodoxy.

First, what are the limits of the grip of constitutional culture? When it comes to the hold that constitutional identity has on political representatives, it is fair to say that Congress is not always mindful of constitutional constraints, least of all when it comes to national security. Invocations of national security increase the likelihood that Congress will take decisions without considering their cost to civil liberty or to separation of powers, in part because they can always say that these considerations are someone else's job—the Supreme Court's. Representatives regularly pass legislation they know will be struck down if challenged in court—like the November 2001 sense of Congress that public schools may display the words "God Bless America" as an expression of support for the nation in this time of emergency. Very few congressional representatives questioned the president's authority to create special military tribunals (and to personally determine who is a terrorist and subject to trial by this court) or, a point on which the executive is legally more vulnerable, the failure to define the category "international terrorist" in a reasonably circumscribed way. Congressional reticence and evasion allow the executive to create the impression that elected representatives have in fact declared war or authorized national security measures when they have not. Congressional inaction invites and provides cover for unilateral executive action. This casts doubt on the suggestion that a good defense against the judiciary's reluctance to independently assess risks to national security is to require congressional authorization for incursions on liberty. Courts would be more protective of civil liberties, on this view, if they struck down particular executive actions that were not supported by unambiguous legislative authorization.[42] The assumption that deliberation by the legislative branch is likely to be more scrupulous about deliberating whether restrictions on liberty are defensible is not confirmed by recent experience. Legislators are not only vulnerable to the same failings in estimating danger, the same susceptibility to fear, as other officials; they also have institutional reasons to want to deflect responsibility.

So a key feature of reason of state in the United States is corrosion of checks and balances: a combination of congressional irresolution, judicial abstention, and presidential defiance.[43] As Justice Jackson acknowledged in *Youngstown,* the president "has the advantage of concentration in a single head in whose choice the whole Nation has a part, making him the focus of public hopes and expectations. In drama, magnitude, and finality his decisions so far overshadow any others that almost alone he fills the public eye and ear."[44] When faced with presidential proposals for statutory changes, political representatives in Congress predictably fail to independently estimate threats to national security or the likely consequences of measures to meet it. One illustration is the infamous bill affirming Japanese American internment despite available information about dissenting views within both the military and the Justice Department. Another familiar case is the Gulf of Tonkin Resolution (which took just forty minutes of discussion in the House).[45] A more recent example is the Republican House version of the 2001 USA Patriot Act, which was written in the middle of the night, without consultation with the Judiciary Committee, and was acquiesced in by Democrats, very few of whom had even read it. Even so, and to the credit of a few adamant representatives, the act took several weeks to pass—more than the three days the angry and impatient attorney general had insisted upon.

Of course, a Congress targeted by suicidal terrorists and criminal anthrax-manufacturers, fearful for its own physical safety, is particularly likely to be deferential toward executive proposals for a Homeland Security agency within the White House, or wiretaps on communications between detainees and counsel, or special military tribunals.

But we should not assume that every concession to "necessity" is the result of disorienting fear untainted by political calculation. Many national security measures are rightly seen as political gesturing at constituents and the press. The motivation is less fear of security than concern for their reelection. Gesturing by political representatives is not costly, indeed it pays dividends when the public itself is ripe for shows of decisive action.

Which leads to the question of constitutional identity among citizens, who must hold officials accountable. Whether it is skin-deep or a constitutive element of American political identity, constitutional commitment is fragile during dangerous times. We have evidence of "soaring popular support for constitutional departures," like the 58 percent who favored more intensive security checks for persons of Arab descent (including American citizens), 49 percent who favored special ID cards for such persons, and 33 percent backing ethnically targeted surveillance.[46] These attitudes are typically explained as the product of fear, never more so than at present. "The analogy between transnational terrorism and immunity-defying viruses has become a commonplace."[47] The analogy is gripping because it says that the killer is invisible, comes to us by stealth, and penetrates within. With fear comes the propensity not to weigh risks against the costs of security measures, but rather to refuse to tolerate risk—to fantasize that risk can be eliminated.

There are exceptions to this analysis of the propensity of fear to license emergency power. Kathleen Sullivan has suggested that we can expect public resistance to universal surveillance. Her explanation is American "quality of life concerns," namely, a deeply held popular presumption in favor of privacy and of individualized rather than general surveillance that makes Americans resistant to surveillance cameras and data collection in public places (and to other aspects of a national security state like identity cards). In fact, evidence suggests that a large swathe of the public now supports these measures. The explanation may not be simply that fear overwhelms constitutional commitments, either. Other, cultural factors may be at work: a lot of blameless Americans feel at home in Panopticon today. Neither Bentham nor Foucault could have foreseen that "life on the screen" would become second nature (nor, for that matter, could they have foreseen the force of narcissism). Americans supportive of privacy-invading technology are not simply resigned to the necessity of security measures or propelled by fear to submit to them; they are comfortable with surveillance. Similarly, there is the techno-attraction of "bionetic" ID cards.

Nonetheless, orthodoxy has it that a frightened public acquiesces in reason of state, and that "Americans are tempted to view the Bill of Rights as a Trojan horse for the enemy."[48] The explanatory emphasis is on fear. What this means, especially once translated into political attitudes and policy, is something of a black box. Unraveling the implications of fear for U.S. policy today, much less the political psychology of fear more broadly, is beyond the scope of this essay. Suffice to say that more than one tradition of political thought proposes fear as the passion to be reckoned with—on the assumption that all times are dangerous times and that fear is a constant element of politics.

Fear can be a basis for political agreement because it is mutually comprehensible. We have all experienced fear and want to avoid it. Fear is the motivation behind Hobbesian political absolutism; the danger of anarchy and war is permanent and should be permanently in our view as a reminder of the obligation to obedience. By contrast, the "liberalism of fear" channels the passion in the direction of vigilance against abuse of power. The experience of official cruelty and oppression works to support limited, liberal government. Notice that in both liberal and absolutist accounts, fear is assumed to be rational, that is, tied to cognitive processes, amenable to revision if the object can be shown to be benign. Fear is the answer to complacency, to political somnambulation.

But there is also what is colloquially described as irrational fear—really paralyzing terror capable of obliterating just about anything from one's mind, certainly sober justifications for constitutional constraints. To be a useful concept, "irrational" fear should not refer to particular objects of terror but to cases where the emotion is unamenable to revision by argument or demonstrations of fact, as in conspiracism or paranoia. Indisputably, the audaciousness of the terrorist attacks of September 11 caused widespread fear that, if dissected, would show both rational insecurity and feverish anxiety, barely suppressed panic. Where threats are plain, enemies stealthy, and security uncertain, nothing is as common as mainstreaming paranoia. Arousing debilitating fear is the whole purpose of terrorism, after all. It seeks to reduce people to a bundle of emotional reactions. It invites irresponsible, impulsive reaction.

The political question is whether fear is exploited by political authorities invoking national security and reason of state. When academic political psychology is not preoccupied with the rational economic choices of individuals, it has focused on popular irrationalism, specifically susceptibility to the political manipulation of fear. Susan Sontag has argued in this vein: "The public is not being asked to bear much of the burden of reality. . . . those in public office have let us know that they consider their task to be a manipulative one: confidence-building and grief management. Politics . . . has been replaced by psychotherapy."[49] Certainly, we are the recipients of ongoing efforts by government officials and professional authorities to name and point up our collective trauma and disorientation and to treat it with "healing" gestures. But that says little about the political intent of policymakers or the effects they have in view. It is hard to tell when security measures are carefully designed for protection and when they are taken for show (either as cynical reassurances or designed to restore a *sense* of security) or, alternatively, when political rhetoric and dramatic measures are meant to keep a sense of insecurity raw and to ward off a return to ordinariness—underscoring our dependence on authority. It is one thing to control access where there is no legitimate and compelling need for general access: controlling weapons on planes, access to the cockpit, and so on. It is another to remove tweezers from travelers' cosmetic kits.

Some observers find a silver lining in fearful readiness to look to government for protection and willingness to trust officials' judgment of necessity. On this sanguine view, fear has dissolved the usual mistrust of government that has supported libertarian and religious conservatism on the one hand and nonideological political disaffection on the other. Fear upends individualism and opens us to a sense of shared fate and community, to a concern for public welfare even if it is costly, and to the benefits of active federal policy. This misbegotten view imagines that attitudes toward national security measures are stable and transferable to other areas of public policy—that it amounts to a generalizable challenge to antigovernmentalism.

The tendency to focus exclusively on fear as the passion to be reckoned with in dangerous times is understandable. It deserves greater study. But as an exclusive focus it is strikingly limited, because it ignores another powerful emotional dynamic at work. That is the thrill of intense energy and direct action—*especially* if it is in response to emergency and takes place outside of or against the law. And especially if it draws on the desire for revenge, which always pushes for direct action and against the rules and restraints of legal due process. Revenge is not rule-bound or orderly; there is a reason we speak of revenge as "wild." Avengers feel perfectly justified in wreaking destruction—they feel liberated to become persecutors in turn. They owe debts to the dead. When it comes to vengeance, generality and proportionality have no place, and cruelty is acceptable. The victims' own perception of affliction, the strength of their passion, their own sense of who is responsible, and the available means of destruction are the only limits.[50] This is captured in the title of a recent article, which characterized presidential military tribunals as "Trial by Fury."[51]

This excited passion, along with fear, is aroused in dangerous times. It fuels reason of state. Above all it supports direct action by political leaders promising swift and strong retaliation. I mention this alternative to fear because it goes to the heart of constitutional reason of state. Justice Brandeis reminded the Court that the constitutional separation of powers was adopted not to promote efficiency but to preclude the exercise of arbitrary power.[52] We also know that impatience with the friction of checks and balances, with the "paralysis" of Congress going about business-as-usual and courts invoking constitutional continuity, is always simmering. It erupts when national security is at issue. President Truman's *Memoirs* is typical in describing congressional deliberation as fatal irresolution: "The Congress was debating and doing a lot of talking about the steel crisis, and I would have welcomed any practical solution from it. But discussion was not enough. I had to act."[53] Defiant presidents challenge ordinary legalism and constitutionalism. President George Bush boasted, "I didn't have to get the permission from some old goat in the United States Congress to kick Saddam Hussein out of Kuwait."[54]

In this connection consider the furious assault on any questioning of presidential action as un-American. In March 2002 Trent Lott lashed out when Senate majority leader Tom Daschle "raised a few mild commonsense cavils about the next stage of the war" (e.g., whom the president was prepared to go to war against, and to what purpose). Lott fired back, "How dare Senator Daschle criticize President Bush while we are fighting our war on terrorism?"[55] This was not calculated to depress serious political opposition (there was none). Its manifest purpose was to impugn patriotism or insufficiently inflamed patriotism. It encouraged unorganized but effective private silencing of questioning and dissent by omnipresent flag-waving and incessant appreciation of heroes. Beyond that is a more comprehensive purpose: aggravating public intolerance of *any check* on emergency action. That is the main point—to inhibit drags on executive action and to make a spectacle of the fact that (right-thinking) congressmen will not be a drag themselves and will put down those who are. It is an exhibition of the passion for direct, aggressive action.

It is no great leap from impatience with checks and balances to outright disgust with constitutionalism. Carl Schmitt expressed this longing exactly: "In the exception, the power of real life breaks through the crust of a mechanism that has become torpid by repetition."[56] Reason of state—whether constitutional dictatorship or prerogative or under cover of constitutional continuity—is seen less as a dangerous solution to a special problem than as an occasion for revivification. It is an opportunity to put an end to ordinariness. Our banal and corrupt personal lives and collective consumer culture can be redeemed by the exception. Nothing deals as fatal a blow to sordid materialism as the need to respond to attacks on national security. Emergency is a testing moment in which we can exhibit our better selves. And our "better self" is not expressed, or not only, in neighborly volunteerism (giving blood, helping out) but in support for and vicarious participation in extraordinary action (like tips to police about suspicious neighbors).[57]

The exhilaration that accompanies aggressive action is the reverse of paralyzing fear. It should not be surprising as a response to terrorism, which is itself, after all, sheer action. Terrorists do not articulate goals. They do not make demands. They are wordless. Striking back, or simply striking out, is experienced as the only emotionally and physiologically satisfying response. Measures that may be effective but preventive are banal—freezing bank accounts, disrupting the flow of funds that allows terrorist groups to recruit. These are not satisfying. A military unleashed promises revenge, though even that may not suffice; witness complaints about the "quagmire" of war or the conflict "bogging down." We should not be blind to this most elementary and damaging face of illiberalism, and this powerful fuel for reason of state: revulsion toward political deliberation, legal due process, and constitutional tests. The last thing many people want is to have responses to the extraordinary represented as ordinary. Or to have "necessity" revealed to be ambiguous, moderate, measured, restrained. Nothing is as insupportable in an agitated state as "suicidal inertia." Even committed liberals warn about "the cognitive and normative analogues to this inertial drag," that is, inflexible attachment to civil liberties.[58] *This,* as much as fear, is the emotional spring, the psychological mechanism behind the political tension of reason of state.

Political psychology argues that the passion to be reckoned with is fear—for reasons that are central to the liberal tradition in particular, where government guarantees of security of life, liberty, and property are an important justification for authority, and where rational fear of government ensures vigilance against abuse of power. Fear is supposed to be the stabilizing touchstone. It can be shattered by crises of national security. In a predictable dynamic, violent assault creates conditions in which illiberal fear crowds out the "liberalism of fear"[59] and invites the cruel necessities of "reason of state." I have suggested that the liberalism of fear—with its horror of official cruelty and vigilance against the powers of government—can be eclipsed by illiberal fear vulnerable to authoritative assertions about what security requires. Constitutional reason of state always threatens to slip from sober calculation of necessary means, reflective fear, into insatiable insecurity.

But powerful as it is, fear is only one of the passions that drive governors to defy constitutional constraints, and citizens to acquiesce. I point to another, overlooked dynamic: the electric jolt of defining enemies and taking (or promising to take) cruel and decisive action. From the regrettable exception we come to frank revulsion at due process and democratic deliberation—to the excited identification of political society with surveillance, force, and punishment. Then, in d'Entreves's words, "Reason of state ended its wretched, precarious existence in council rooms and came out into the open to be hailed as the very 'soul of the state.'"[60]

CONCLUSION

The thrust of this essay is the limitation of formal constitutionalism as a way of understanding and assessing reason of state. Constitutional constraints are potentially important, particularly when "constitutional culture" and "constitutional identity" are intact. But none of the three constitutional models—emergency dictatorship, prerogative, or continuous constitutionalism—is a guaranteed brake on runaway emergency powers. With reason of state we reach the boundary of legalism. Reason of state poses an enduring *political* puzzle. In thinking about constraints on reason of state, extraconstitutional considerations are crucial. I focused on three: recognition of the enduring nature of emergency legislation; the looseness in government created by federalism and localism; and the associations of civil society designed to investigate and publicize abuse of power.

Underlying all of these, and at the heart of reason of state, is the political psychology that makes democratic citizens vulnerable to pronouncements of "necessity." The orthodox view is that fear is the passion to be reckoned with, and it is. I have argued that we must acknowledge fear's passionate twin—the latent hunger for aggressive action brought to the surface by the perception of threat and even more by actual aggression. This psychology can only be satisfied by precisely those measures that burst the bounds of law and exhibit the desired transcendence of ordinary for extraordinary times.

NOTES

An earlier version of this essay was delivered as a commentary on the Tanner Lectures at Harvard University, "Civil Liberties during Wartime," delivered by Kathleen Sullivan, November 2001.

1. Kathleen Sullivan, "War, Peace, and Civil Liberties: Constitutionalism," The Tanner Lectures, Harvard University, November 2001 (unpublished lectures).
2. This is one formulation of reason of state. Another is that it severs the factual demands of a given situation and moral judgment passed on them. Cf. Alexander Passerin d'Entreves, *The Notion of the State* (Oxford: Clarendon Press, 1967), 45.
3. Michael Harrington, cited in Carl Friedrich, *Constitutional Reason of State* (Providence: Brown University, 1957), 119.
4. It is resonant of Socrates' question, which Wendy Brown recalls in her essay: does this political order continue to have a claim to our love?
5. Cited in Jules Lobel, "Emergency Power and the Decline of Liberalism," 98 *Yale Law Journal* 1385 (1989): 1393.
6. Cited in David Bonner, *Emergency Powers in Peacetime* (London: Sweet and Maxwell, 1985), 2.

7. Philip B. Heymann, "Terrorism, Freedom, and Security," unpublished paper in possession of the author.

8. Machiavelli, *Discourses on Livy*, I, 34 in *The Prince and the Discourses* (New York: Random House, 1950), 203.

9. Carl Schmitt, *Political Theology*, cited in John P. McCormick, *Carl Schmitt's Critique of Liberalism* (Cambridge: Cambridge University Press, 1997), 133.

10. See, for example, the discussions in David Bonner, *Emergency Powers in Peacetime* (London: Sweet and Maxwell, 1985), and Laura K. Donohue, *Counter-Terrorist Law and Emergency Powers in the United Kingdom, 1922–2000* (Dublin: Irish Academic Press, 2001).

11. *Youngstown Sheet and Tube v. Sawyer* 343 U.S. 579 (1952); dialogue is from oral argument before the District Court for D.C. cited in Clinton Rossiter, *The Supreme Court and the Commander in Chief* (Ithaca: Cornell University Press, 1976), xix.

12. *Youngstown Sheet and Tube Co. v. Sawyer* 343 U.S. 579 (1952).

13. Cited in Lobel, "Emergency Power," 1407 n. 108.

14. John Locke, *Two Treatises of Government*, edited by Peter Laslett (Cambridge: Cambridge University Press, 1960), 375.

15. John Hart Ely opposes this position but discusses the view of some of the founders that "under emergency conditions the executive can properly act in excess of legislative authorization, so long as he makes a swift and full disclosure to the legislature and subsides if they do not approve." *War and Responsibility: Constitutional Lessons of Vietnam and Its Aftermath* (Princeton: Princeton University Press, 1993), 7.

16. Rossiter, *Supreme Court*, 29.

17. *Korematsu v. U.S.* 323 U.S. 214 (1944): 243–48.

18. *Ex Parte Milligan*, 71 U.S. 2 (1866).

19. Kathleen Sullivan, "War, Peace, and Civil Liberties: American Identity," unpublished Tanner Lecture.

20. For a discussion see Christopher N. May, *In the Name of War: Judicial Review and the War Powers since 1918* (Cambridge: Harvard University Press, 1989).

21. See *Ex Parte Merryman*, 17 F. Cas. 144 (1861) and *Ex parte Milligan*, 71 U.S. 2 (1866).

22. For an extended discussion that includes Justice Jackson's classification of the authoritativeness of presidential actions, see Alan F. Westin, *The Anatomy of a Constitutional Law Case: Youngstown Sheet and Tube Co. v. Sawyer, The Steel Seizure Decision* (New York: Columbia University Press, 1958).

23. *Kennedy v. Mendoza-Martinez*, 372 U.S. 144 (1963), 159–60.

24. Sullivan, "War, Peace, and Civil Liberties: Constitutionalism," unpublished Tanner Lecture.

25. In *Schenck v. U.S.*, 249 U.S. 47 (1919); *Debs v. U.S.*, 249 (U.S. 211 (1919) and *Abrams v. U.S.*, 250 U.S. 616 (1919). The literature on these speech cases is an ongoing cottage industry. The most protective statement, still law, is *Brandenburg v. Ohio*, 395 U.S. 444 (1969). See David Cole's essay in this volume for a full discussion.

26. See *Hirabayashi v. U.S.*, 320 U.S. 81 (1943) and *Korematsu v. U.S.*, 323 U.S. 213 (1944). The decision was particularly egregious because Congress had access from the Justice Department and the military indicating that neither entity believed General DeWitt's claims of the military necessity for relocation.

27. Attorney General Francis Biddle, cited in Sullivan, "War, Peace, and Civil Liberties: Constitutionalism," unpublished Tanner Lecture, 11.

28. Cited in Jeffrey Toobin, "Crackdown," *New Yorker*, November 5, 2001, 60.

29. Some of these are discussed in Kathleen Sullivan, "War, Peace, and Civil Liberties: American Identity," the Tanner Lectures at Harvard University, November 2001 (unpublished paper). This still falls short of British and Israeli legislation on terrorism as special paramilitary actors treated differentially within the civilian system.

30. Rossiter, *Supreme Court*, 127.

31. William J. Brennan Jr., "The Quest to Develop a Jurisprudence of Civil Liberties in Times of Security Crises," delivered December 22, 1987, Law School of Hebrew University, Jerusalem, Israel, 8.

32. The phrase is from Ernst Fraenkel, *The Dual State: A Contribution to the Theory of Dictatorship* (New York: Oxford, 1941). Fraenkel speaks of normative and prerogative systems of law under National Socialism and concludes: "Every nation would allow that there are emergencies in which it is the right and duty of government to proclaim a state of siege and authorize the suppression of the common rules of remedy by the rapid methods of martial law. What Machiavelli did, or what his follower have been doing ever since, is to elevate this principle into the normal rule for statesmen's actions." By citing this I do not mean to suggest that reason of state is an inevitable decline into Nazism.

33. The little known Surveillance Court instituted in the 1970s by the Foreign Intelligence Surveillance Act and reaffirmed by the USA Patriot Act whose purpose is to rule on foreign intelligence wiretaps and searches without a showing of probable cause required by criminal warrants. It remains to see if this authority is now extended to American citizens of foreign descent or affiliation.

34. Friedrich, *Constitutional Reason of State*, 115.

35. Friedrich, *Constitutional Reason of State*, 11.

36. Arthur Schlesinger Jr., "A Democrat Looks at Foreign Policy," *Foreign Affairs* 66, no. 2 (winter 1987–88): 263–83, quotations at 265, 277, 281.

37. Christopher May, *In the Name of War: Judicial Review and the War Powers since 1918* (Cambridge: Harvard University Press, 1989), 254.

38. See the discussion of a permanent emergency beginning in 1950 in Lobel, "Emergency Power," 1400ff.

39. Cited in Toobin, "Crackdown," 56, 58.

40. Deborah Sontag, "Who Is This Kafka That People Keep Mentioning," *New York Times Magazine*, October 21, 2001, 57.

41. ACLU Washington Update, Phil Gutis, October 30, 2000 (internal email communication to state affiliates). These findings are explained and confirmed

in W. Ip Viscusi and Richard J. Zeckhauser, "Sacrificing Civil Liberties to Reduce Terrorism Risks," unpublished paper on file with the author.

42. Cass Sunstein, "Fear and Liberty," *Social Research* (forthcoming).

43. Ely, *War and Responsibility,* an extended study of "Congress's penchant for studied ambiguity," 12.

44. Cited in Westin, *Anatomy of a Constitutional Law Case,* 155.

45. Ely, *War and Responsibility,* 19.

46. Cited in Sullivan, "War, Peace, and Civil Liberties: Constitutionalism," 4.

47. Stephen Holmes, "Liberalism in the Mirror of Transnational Terror," *Tocqueville Review* 22, no. 2 (2001): 5–35, quotation at 7.

48. Holmes, "Liberalism," 13.

49. Susan Sontag, "Talk of the Town: Tuesday and After," *New Yorker,* September 24, 2001, 32.

50. See Nancy L. Rosenblum, "The Experience of Injustice" in Martha Minow and Nancy L. Rosenblum, *Breaking the Cycles of Vengeance: Memory, Law, and Repair* (Princeton: Princeton University Press, 2002).

51. Laurence H. Tribe, "Why Congress Must Curb Bush's Military Courts: Trial by Fury," *New Republic online:* www.tnr.com/121001/tribe121001.html, 1. Though even military tribunals retain more of the apparatus of legalism than many would prefer.

52. *Myers v. U.S.* 272 U.S. 52, 240, cited in Westin, *Anatomy of a Constitutional Law Case,* 147.

53. Westin, *Anatomy of a Constitutional Law Case,* 13.

54. Cited in Ely, *War and Responsibility,* 1.

55. Cited in Frank Rich, "The Wimps of War," *New York Times,* March 30, 2002, A27.

56. *Political Theology* (Cambridge: MIT Press, 1985), 15.

57. This need not entail the Schmitt/Benjamin/Sorel preoccupation with myth (specifically the myth of an existentially threatening other) or their profound illiberalism. See Jan-Werner Muller, "Myth, Law, and Order: Schmitt and Benjamin Read *Reflections on Violence,*" unpublished paper in possession of the author.

58. Holmes, "Liberalism," 21.

59. "Liberalism of fear" is Judith Shklar's name for a variant of liberalism that emphasizes checks on government motivated by historical experience of cruelty and abuse, in Nancy L. Rosenblum, ed., *Liberalism and the Moral Life* (Cambridge: Harvard University Press, 1989).

60. D'Entreves, *Notion of the State,* 47.

CONTRIBUTORS

Lauren Berlant, Professor of English, University of Chicago

Wendy Brown, Professor of Political Science, University of California, Berkeley

David Cole, Professor of Law, Georgetown Law Center

Hugh Gusterson, Associate Professor of Anthropology, Massachusetts Institute of Technology

Nancy L. Rosenblum, Senator Joseph Clark Professor of Ethics in Politics and Government, Harvard University

Austin Sarat, William Nelson Cromwell Professor of Jurisprudence and Political Science, Amherst College

INDEX